Judy

Judy

Portrait of an American Legend

Thomas J. Watson
and
Bill Chapman

McGraw-Hill Book Company

New York   St. Louis   San Francisco
Hamburg   Mexico   Toronto

For Edna M. Watson
and in memory of Donald C., who gave me
the courage to dream.

T.J.W.

For Winnie Rose Chapman,
who would have loved it—and for
my friends through the years,
Bob Main, Jim Breen, and
Peter Machaverna.

B.C.

CREDITS

Grateful acknowledgment is made to George Hurrell for permission to reprint the portrait on page 3 of the color section, and to the late John Engstead for the photographs on the frontispiece page, the page facing page 1, and those on pages 34, 50, 62, 70, 76, 78, 98. Other photo credits: Acme Photo, 65, 68; *American Weekly*, 72; Arcola Music, Inc., 114; Arsene Studio, 84; Associated Press, 23, 27, 68; Capitol Records Industries, 108; CBS, Inc., 44, 100, 102; Central Press Association, 104; Pat Clark, 72; Leo Feist, Inc., 17; Globe Photos, 109; Harwin Music Corp., 96; Impact Photos, Inc., 113; International News Photo, 75; King Features Syndicate, 19, 23; *Ladies' Home Journal*, 40; Lancaster, California, *Ledger-Gazette*, 5; Gene Lester, 39; *London Daily Express*, 90; Metro-Goldwyn-Mayer, 22, 37, 39, 54, 56–7, 59; NBC, 57, 110; *Paris Match*, 90; *Philadelphia Daily News*, 95, 100; *Pictorial Parade*, 52; Time-Life, Inc., 47; United Artists Corporation, 92, 94; United Press International Photo, 91, 111, 112, 114, 115; United Press Telephoto, 81, 110, 112; United States Navy, 70; Warner Bros. Pictures, Inc., 73, 75; Dick Whittington, 11; Wide World Photo, 70, 100.

All photographs from the collection of Bill Chapman

1 2 3 4 5 6 7 8 9 HAL HAL 8 7 6

ISBN 0-07-068487-1

LIBRARY OF CONGRESS CATALOGING-IN-PUBLICATION DATA

Watson, Thomas, 1948–
Judy: portrait of an American legend.
Includes index.
1. Garland, Judy.   2. Singers—United States—
Biography.   3. Moving-picture actors and actresses—
United States—Biography.   I. Chapman, Bill.   II. Title.
ML420.G253W4   1986   784.5′0092′4 [B]   85-19860
ISBN 0-07-068487-1

Book design by Kathryn Parise

ACKNOWLEDGMENTS

No one has ever had fans the way Judy Garland has fans, and we feel privileged to count many of Judy's staunchest admirers among our closest associates. Together we wish to thank Jim Breen, John Behrens, John Fricke, Les Perkins, and Ron O'Brien for their generous assistance and constant enthusiasm for all things Judy.

We would also like to thank Franciene Wilkins, for helping us secure and identify Judy's beautiful John Engstead portraits; George Hurrell, for allowing us to reproduce his wonderful color portrait of Judy; and Earl E. Atwater. Grateful appreciation is also extended to Betty Reed, for supplying information regarding Judy's appearances on NBC, and to Ken Sephton of the Judy Garland Fan Club (London).

Mr. Chapman extends a note of thanks to Arthur Ruiz, Virginia Back and Michael Back, Sue Saper, Unity, Dore Freeman, Pam Wulk, Wilbur George, Ed Baker, Talbert Kanniger, Jason Ross, Myron Braum, Peter Bateman, the late Bob Chatterton, Wayne Lawless, Sidney Seigel, Leonard Sergio, Bob Main, Peter Machaverna, Frank Wolshon, Roy Bishop, Ken Galente, Joe Di Marino, and, especially, Lou Valentino.

Mr. Watson wishes to thank Rick Carl, Mark Towner, Dave Woodman, Betty White, and Lynn Becker and Arnold Becker for their friendship and support and for understanding why, during a project such as this, the phone seldom rings. Special gratitude must go to Richard Brock, whose love and trust and companionship make great challenges possible.

Finally, we wish to thank our agents, Bart Andrews and Sherry Robb, for believing in us, our book designer, Kathryn Parise, and our editor, Thomas Ward Miller, for offering constant support and creative insights.

Without such people, no project is possible . . . or worthwhile.

1

With her life, as with her song,
she gave us love—and hope.
ADELA ROGERS ST. JOHNS

houghts of Judy Garland almost automatically conjure up one of two images. One image is a consummate concert artist—a woman standing in a spotlight at the end of a runway, one hand clutching a microphone while the other flails wildly in time with the music; the other is a character from a decades-old but still popular movie—perhaps little Dorothy skipping down a yellow-brick road, Judy and Mickey Rooney putting on a show, or Esther Blodgett lamenting the man that got away.

Judy was all these images and more. During a career that spanned nearly forty-five years, she mastered every conceivable medium—vaudeville, motion pictures, records, radio, television, nightclubs, and the concert stage. She was an actress, dancer, gifted comedienne, and, most of all, singer. "All I ever really wanted to do was sing," she often confessed, and audiences all over the world let her. "She's a songwriter's dream," commented America's most prolific tunesmith, Irving Berlin. "I'll go on record as saying that."

Such words of praise were commonplace for Judy Garland, who received critical acclaim during her whole career, beginning with the chorus of "Jingle Bells" that she sang at age two and a half, from the stage of her father's movie theatre on December 26, 1924, in Grand Rapids, Minnesota.

Even at the age of one, Judy, née Frances Gumm, was ready to smile for the camera.

Judy's parents, Frank and Ethel Gumm, were "theatre folk" in the small-time vaudeville sense. They had met at the Savoy Theatre in Superior, Wisconsin, where he was singing and she working as the house pianist. The Gumms were married in January 1914, and, although they contemplated a career on the road, they soon settled in Grand Rapids. Frank signed on to manage the local New Grand Theatre, and Ethel agreed to provide accompaniment for both live artists and silent films.

The Gumms discovered a way to have both a career in show business and a stable home life. In September 1915, their first daughter, Mary Jane, was born; in July 1917, Dorothy Virginia. In the fall of 1921, Ethel became pregnant a third time; although she did not especially want another child, her doctors advised against any sort of abortion. Frances Ethel Gumm, named for both her parents—but destined to be Judy Garland—was born on June 10, 1922.

By the time "Baby" (a nickname Frank had once been called) Frances was two years old, the Gumms were well established as celebrities in Grand Rapids. Whenever a function called for entertainment, Frank, Ethel, Mary Jane, and Virginia were asked to per-

form. In the spring of 1924, Baby joined the act, singing at a local dry goods company fashion show, and on Christmas of that year she made her theatrical debut. She later recalled:

"Jingle Bells," the first song I sang on a stage, taught me one of the most important rules of theatre: knowing when to get off. I was nearly three years old at the time, and Dad finally succumbed to my pleas to let me sing on amateur night in his theatre. I was too young to be scared, and in a loud voice I sang the chorus of "Jingle Bells." I was supposed to bow and leave the stage at the finish, but I guess the ham in me had been aroused, for I went right on singing the chorus over and over. Finally Dad marched out on the stage and carried me off, kicking and squealing. The family took turns in explaining how to end an act despite applause. I learned that lesson well, and to this day whenever an enthusiastic audience gives me that "wanting to sing all night" feeling, I hear the first notes of "Jingle Bells" and make a quick exit.

Not all the Gumm girls' life was built around show business. For the most part, they had a normal small-midwestern-town childhood. Virginia later remembered Baby Frances as "a quiet child. She played a lot by herself, liked to model clays, had the usual number of dolls, all of which were called Peggy! She seemed older than her age and was very sensitive. Her outstanding quality was her fundamental seriousness. She was dreamy, too. I caught her a few times standing before the mirror and applying rouge to her cheeks to make her look more sophisticated. I am five years older, but I hardly ever felt the difference in our ages."

During the spring of 1926, as Baby was nearing her fourth birthday, Frank and Ethel decided to take a "working vacation," a trip to the west coast. Ethel later recalled that the original plan called for the girls to stay at home with their grandmother—but three sad faces changed everything. "I was packing the day before we were to leave, and there they stood watching, and all of a sudden I looked up at them and knew I couldn't leave them. So I chased downtown, picked up three pairs of overalls and some middies, and we took them along and had a wonderful time."

Leaving Grand Rapids June 8, the Gumms, traveling professionally as "Jack and Virginia Lee, and Three Little Lees," worked their way across Montana, Idaho, and into Washington. Virginia later explained the informality of it all: "We'd stop in a town and my daddy'd go to the newspaper, or to the theatre owner, and offer to play a show that night. That's the way things were done then."

Judy later recalled that vaudeville was on its last legs in 1926, and that it was acts like the Gumms' that finally killed it. Except for her father, she remarked:

It was a lousy act. My father had a wonderful voice, but my mother didn't sing well . . . and we kids were terrible, too. We appeared separately. First we'd sit out front and applaud for Mother and Daddy, and then they'd do the same for us when we were onstage. After Mother and Father's act, she'd dash into the pit to play the piano, and he would dress us in our costumes backstage. I did those horrible Egyptian bellyrolls, in an Egyptian outfit with those big balloon pants and a lot of ankle bracelets and spangles.

The Gumms spent a few days that summer in Seattle and then took a train to Portland, where Frank showed his family the sights. Then a boat trip to San Francisco, after which the Gumms headed for Los Angeles. A few friends from Grand Rapids had already migrated there.

During their ten days in Hollywood, the Gumms saw all the traditional sights and visited various movie studios. "We walked our fool heads off," is the way Ethel later put it. "We camped on the front lawn of the old Warner studio on Sunset and watched the movie stars come out. Of course, we wanted to see them!"

Judy later reported that she "made her radio debut in Los Angeles at the age of four," which would indicate that the Gumms also performed in some capacity while in the Hollywood area that summer.

Although show business opportunities excited them, what Frank and Ethel really liked was the southern California climate. Remembering the deadly cold Minnesota winters, Ethel told reporters, "We came to California to get away from the coal bills and the storm windows. This was the place, we decided. Back we went, sold the theatre, and packed up our goods and our youngsters."

Actually, it took the family nearly four months to tie up their affairs in Grand Rapids, and another three or four to get themselves established in California. They had dreamed of setting themselves up with a business much the way they had in Minnesota, but, as Ethel explained, "we found on returning that most of the Los Angeles theatres were owned by the big chains—and so we finally bought a theatre in the little desert town of Lancaster, and settled down to living."

Frank immediately refurbished the establishment, renamed it the Valley Theatre, added a ticket booth

Judy, at three, could sing and be heard in the back of a theatre.

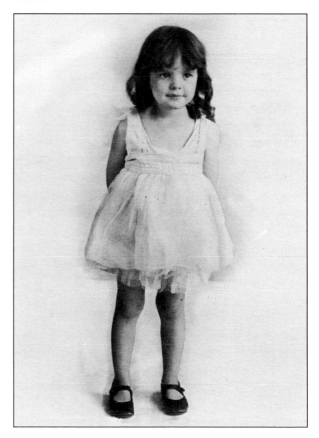

3

The Gumms circulated this photo while living at 1207 Cedar Street in Lancaster, California. Their phone number: Lancaster 1101.

and air conditioning, and booked his own family to perform between pictures. Lancaster welcomed them with open arms, and the whole family was quickly assimilated into the community.

"Babe," as Frances was now called, made over a dozen appearances at her father's theatre during 1927 and 1928 and, in August 1928, while Ethel and the girls were vacationing in Santa Monica, appeared on KFI radio's *Kiddies Hour*.

Frequent 60-mile trips between Lancaster and Los Angeles followed, and, by Christmas, all three Gumm daughters had joined Ethel Meglin's *Meglin Kiddie Review*, which had been booked for a two-week holiday run at the Loews State Theatre in downtown Los Angeles.

Despite later reports to the contrary, neither Frank nor Ethel was shoving the girls into show business. They were eager to enter the family business, and their careers were evolving under their own momentum.

Between January 1929 and August 1933, the Gumms lived apart as much as they did together. Frank maintained his little theatre in Lancaster, while Ethel and the girls scurried back and forth to Los Angeles. In June 1929, the girls made their motion-picture debut in a talkie short subject, *The Big Review*, featuring all the Meglin kiddies. By the fall of 1929, the girls had joined yet another group of youngsters, billed as the "Hollywood Starlets."

More film shorts followed (*Holiday in Storyland, The Wedding of Jack and Jill, Bubbles*), and, in July

1931, the girls were featured in producer Maurice Kusell's *Stars of Tomorrow* review at the Wilshire Ebell Theatre. In January and March of 1932, Babe, now nearly ten, made two solo appearances during special "Star Night" programs at the Cocoanut Grove.

The production and management team of Fanchon and Marco, who had produced the lavish Loews State live presentations, booked the Gumms for a number of appearances at movie houses throughout southern California during the summer of 1932, and the following winter Babe appeared solo at both the fancy Fox Arlington Theatre in Santa Barbara and the Million Dollar Theatre in downtown Los Angeles. By January 1933, Ethel was making plans to relocate herself and the girls to L.A. permanently.

Judy, at age seven, performed on stages in and around Los Angeles.

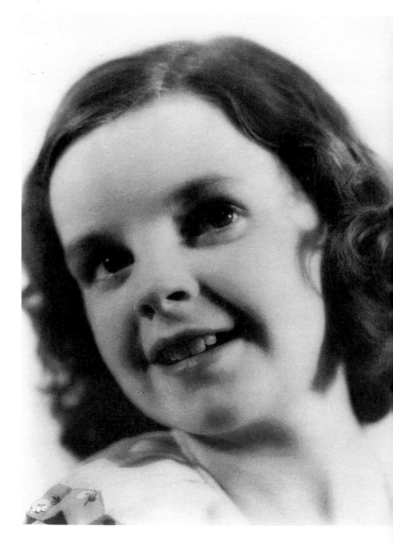

Baby Frances makes news in the Lancaster *Ledger-Gazette* in 1931.

Babe made many solo appearances in and around Los Angeles that spring; in early summer all three girls became regulars on KFWB radio's *Junior Hi-Jinx Hour*. Bookings at the RKO Hillstreet followed, and later the girls traveled to San Francisco, where they were booked into the Golden Gate Theatre. Judy would later look back on this trip with fondness; it introduced her to another family of vaudevillians, the O'Connors. She and young Donald O'Connor (three years her junior) would remain friends for life.

Frank Gumm joined his family in Los Angeles in August 1933, and the family rented a house in the Silver Lake area just east of Hollywood. Babe was delighted to have her father home: "My father and I were very close," she later explained. "He loved music and the theatre and everything about it. He

sort of planted it in me!" Frank, however, still owned the Valley Theatre in Lancaster, and he spent much of his time there managing it.

Babe and Virginia were enrolled at Viola "Mom" Lawlor's School for Professional Children, located next door to the central casting offices at the corner of Sunset and Western. Babe's classmates included Joe Yule (whose professional name was Mickey Rooney), Dawn O'Day (Anne Shirley), and Frankie Darrow. Mickey later recalled, "I remember the day I met this girl. Frances Gumm—how could I forget a name like that. I went home that day and told my mom, 'I met a girl today named Frances Gumm . . . she was kinda sticky!' The joke didn't go over so well then, either."

By 1934, Shirley Temple, a former Lawlor student, was the biggest name in pictures, and studio talent scouts were always on the lookout for new talent. During the spring of 1934, a scout from Universal put all three Gumm girls under option for a new movie they were preparing, an elaborate biography of showman Florenz Ziegfeld. The project was budgeted at far more money than Universal was ultimately prepared to pay, and after months of development the studio sold the property to MGM. The Gumm sisters were not included in the sale.

In June, the Gumms decided to visit the Century of Progress exposition in Chicago. Ethel and the

The Gumm Sisters make their film debut with the Meglin Kiddies in *The Big Revue* in 1929.

girls left Los Angeles June 18. Arriving in Denver, they worked a week in a nightclub. A booking in Colorado Springs followed; the Gumms finally arrived in Chicago in mid-July. They found employment at a restaurant near the Fair called the Old Mexico Cafe for $35 per week. They worked three weeks, got paid for one, and found themselves out of a job when the establishment went out of business. The Gumms stayed on in an inexpensive show-business hotel and appeared one night as a fill-in act at the Belmont Theatre.

A few days later, while Ethel was packing for the trip home, the girls received a call from musician Jack Cathcart, who had seen their act at the Belmont. Cathcart, who would later marry Mary Jane, had just discovered a vacancy on the bill at the Oriental Theater. Could the Gumms come over right away to audition? The booking would be for only five days—but it would be on a bill headed by the great Georgie Jessel. The girls jumped at the chance!

The Gumms got the job. Babe wowed the audience with her emotional rendition of Helen Morgan's "Bill."

The whole family was dismayed to hear the audience laugh when they were introduced as the Glum Sisters. After the second show, Jessel advised, "You have to change your name."

"To what?" the girls asked.

"I don't know. I'll do it."

Virginia later said, "Between shows Jessel got a long-distance call from Robert Garland. We were standing in the wings for the third show, and he introduced us as 'the Garland Sisters.' . . . And it didn't get a laugh, so we just kept it."

The Garlands (Mary Jane, now nearly nineteen; Virginia, seventeen; and Babe, twelve) were a great success. Doors started opening. They did a week in Detroit, in Milwaukee, and in a few other cities, and then they headed for home. "We'd had enough," said Ethel. "We'd proved our point. We were all terribly homesick for Frank, so we piled into the car and went back where we belonged."

Back in California, the Garland Sisters worked regularly, appearing for a week at Grauman's Chinese Theatre in Los Angeles and making excursions to San Francisco and Long Beach.

In December, Babe landed a screen test at Metro-Goldwyn-Mayer. *Variety* reported, "Metro tested Frances Garland, a twelve-year-old, for a featured part in *Broadway Melody*. Youngster, with her two sisters, has played locally for several years as the Gumm Sisters, singing trio. Lately, she has been featured with trio as a mimic." The part went to someone else.

In April 1935, Frank finally sold his theatre in Lancaster and bought a new one in the Los Angeles suburb of Lomita. Both he and Ethel adopted "Garland" as their new family name, and, on June 8, the girls performed for the first time at Garland's Lomita Theatre.

The girls decided to try new first names as well. Babe decided to call herself "Judy," after the famous song by Hoagy Carmichael; Mary Jane became Susie; Virginia became Jimmie.

During June and July, the newly named trio was booked for what would become a six-week working vacation at Bones Remer's Cal-Neva Lodge in Lake Tahoe. "That's the place," Judy recalled later, "where the state line runs right through the middle of the dance floor. At that time, if you sat on one side of the dining room, you paid a sales tax; on the other side, you didn't. During our act Jimmie and I would wave to each other from different states."

During the course of the booking, Mary Jane/Susie met and fell in love with a young musician playing in the band, Lee Kahn. They planned to be married in August. Virginia also expressed hopes of marrying and settling down, leading Judy and Ethel to believe that if they were to continue the act, it would have to be as a single.

The day the Garlands were leaving Tahoe, Judy auditioned for songwriter Harry Akst, who promised to get her in to see casting directors at the major Hollywood studios. Judy's version of the day went like this:

I've heard about twenty versions of what happened next, some of them pretty wild. One story has it that MGM signed me without a screen or sound test. Nothing could be further from the truth. We went home to a house we'd taken in

Los Angeles, and a few days later Lew Brown, the songwriter, who was also an executive at Columbia Pictures, called up and asked my mother to bring me to the studio. He'd been at Bones' table with Harry Akst. Of course, we went, and I sang for some people there, but nobody was impressed. Lew Brown told an agent named Al Rosen about me, and Al towed me all over southern California. I think I had an audition at every major studio, but everyone kept saying, "She isn't any age. She isn't a child wonder, and she isn't grown up." Nobody had ever heard of "Junior Miss" or "Corliss Archer" then. A teenager was regarded as a menace to the industry and fit only to be stuffed in a barrel until she could be made into a glamour job.

The three Garland Sisters did get one final appearance together in another film short, Lewis Lewin's *La Fiesta de Santa Barbara*.

Judy started back to school and was booked by Rosen to sing at the Wilshire Ebell Theatre. Unbeknownst to either of them, people were beginning to talk about this young girl with the grown-up voice. Joe Mankiewicz, an MGM writer-producer, heard Judy sing at the Ebell and mentioned her name to Ida Koverman, executive assistant to Metro studio chief Louis B. Mayer. Koverman remembered Mankiewicz's enthusiasm when Rosen called a few days

later to try to arrange an audition. Koverman agreed to hear the child.

Judy later recalled the day (September 13, 1935) that Rosen called with the good news: "My agent called me and said he wanted to take me to MGM. For once my mother wasn't home to go with me. My father went with us. Well, I thought, another old studio! I had on a pair of old slacks and an old polo shirt and I just went the way I was."

Rosen and Koverman, of course, were more interested in the way Judy sounded than in how she looked. With Frank at the piano, Judy sang a new song, "Zing! Went the Strings of My Heart." She was nervous, and Frank's piano technique left much to be desired, adding to his daughter's shaky performance. Koverman summoned studio arranger Roger Edens to relieve Frank and asked music publisher Jack Robbins to sit in. This time Judy was note perfect, and a third performance was requested for the ears of L. B. Mayer himself. A few days later, Judy was given a contract.

The exact sequence of events leading up to Judy's arrival at Metro-Goldwyn-Mayer has been blurred by time and legend. Some historians say she was not required to make a screen test; others insist she was. Whatever the studio required of her, she passed muster. All the years of hard work, of singing in small towns on the outskirts of show business, had finally paid off. She was on her way!

OVERLEAF: The Gumm Sisters, 1931.

7

Judy Garland was a little Mozart of song and dance.
BUDD SHULBERG

In 1935, Metro-Goldwyn-Mayer (MGM) was the quintessential Hollywood studio—a class act. It boasted "More Stars Than There Are in Heaven"; when Judy joined the studio it had Joan Crawford, Clark Gable, Greta Garbo, Norma Shearer, Jeanette MacDonald, Nelson Eddy, Spencer Tracy, William Powell, Myrna Loy, Jean Harlow, and the Marx Brothers under contract.

Under Louis B. Mayer, MGM provided everything imaginable to contract performers: singing, dancing, and acting lessons; makeup artists; beauticians; doctors; dentists; and especially public relations experts. Each career was carefully crafted; nothing was left to chance. To be under contract at MGM meant that one had "made it" in Hollywood.

Judy's contract, signed September 27, 1935, and approved in Superior Court on October 15, was a standard seven-year pact, starting at $150 per week with escalations leading up to an eventual weekly salary of $1000.

Her first few months at MGM were a period of trial and error. The studio was not exactly sure what to do with her. She came under the tutelage of MGM's resident musical arranger and vocal coach, Roger Edens, the man who had relieved Frank at the piano during her audition. "Lord, what a sweet girl Judy was!"

Edens recalled later. "Bright. Cheerful. So anxious to please. So eager to work. Couldn't read music, but she didn't have to. Her talent was inborn. She had a perfect anatomy for a singer, built around a super muscle of a diaphragm. Her voice was a completely natural and beautiful instrument. She had a wonderful memory. What could I teach her? How to sing a lyric. How to get the meaning across."

Edens was so impressed by his first sessions with Judy that he recommended her for an appearance on *Shell Chateau*, a Saturday-night variety hour on NBC Radio. Judy's performance October 26 proved so successful that the producers asked her back for the broadcast of November 16.

Judy was in particularly fine voice that November night—she was singing for her father. Frank had become ill the night before with a chronic inner-ear infection, and he had been rushed to Cedars of Lebanon Hospital. Marc Rabwin, the family doctor, called Judy at the station and told her that a radio had been placed at Frank's bedside so that he would not miss her program.

The next day, on Ethel's thirty-ninth birthday, Frank died. His ear infection had drained into his body, bringing on a virulent type of spinal meningitis. His death was very traumatic for Judy, who later confessed, "I couldn't cry for eight days. . . . Then I locked myself in a bathroom and cried for fourteen hours." She started looking for reminders of Frank in every man she met. It would become a lifelong pursuit.

Victor Young, orchestra leader on *Shell Chateau*, knew a good voice when he heard it. After Judy's two performances on his program, he mentioned her name to friends at Decca Records. On November 27, she cut two "test" sides for them. Neither song was released, but the audition session laid the groundwork for Judy's later ten-year contract with Decca.

Roger Edens said of Judy's early months at MGM: "She went to school on the lot and worked with us after school hours. Each session lasted at least an hour. Often she'd stay two hours, three hours, and I'd have to make her go home."

By spring, Judy was being considered for parts in *This Time It's Love*, a proposed Robert Montgomery picture, and *Born to Dance*, producer Jack Cum-

mings' latest Eleanor Powell musical, but neither job materialized.

In June, MGM sent Judy and Ethel to New York on a "working birthday holiday." Ida Koverman provided letters of introduction to MGM's New York office, which arranged for Judy to sing on WHN, Metro's Manhattan radio station. On June 12, she visited Decca Records' New York studios and, with the Bob Crosby Orchestra, cut two songs—"Swing Mr. Charlie" and "Stompin' at the Savoy."

Back in Los Angeles, Louis B. Mayer sat worried. He had heard the high praise various executives had showered on Judy, but he also knew the studio was paying her over $150 per week and had as yet been unable to find a single film for her to do.

Judy's contract, ostensibly for seven years, included a standard "bailout" clause, enabling MGM to release her at the end of any six-month period. With option time approaching in September, Mayer wanted action. He asked producer Jack Chertok to come up with some sort of quickie short subject that would let him see exactly how Judy Garland looked and sounded on the screen.

Judy at Los Angeles Superior Court signs her first contract with MGM in 1935.

Judy joins Wallace Beery and Jackie Cooper on NBC's *Shell Chateau* radio show in 1935.

Chertok concocted *Every Sunday* (also known as *Every Sunday Afternoon*), in which Judy and another young contract player, Deanna Durbin, would appear as friends at Sunday afternoon band concerts. Judy sang jazz, Deanna, classical music. The whole production was planned and filmed in less than two weeks. Mayer was satisfied with both girls' performances—in fact, he was dismayed to learn that Durbin had already gotten away. Her contract had lapsed, and she had been snapped up to star in *Three Smart Girls* at Universal.

Judy's reaction to *Every Sunday* was more critical than Mayer's: "I thought I would photograph like a siren. And when I saw a chubby, freckle-faced, snub-nosed little girl on the screen, and I realized I was looking at myself, I went home and cried myself to sleep."

Judy was no great beauty in 1936, but neither was she the ugly duckling she thought herself to be. Part of the problem was that at the studio she was constantly surrounded by some of the most beautiful women in the world and she no longer had her father to baby her and reinforce a positive self-image.

MGM still had no feature film in mind for Judy, but 20th Century-Fox, a new studio less than a year old, did. Producer Darryl F. Zanuck asked to borrow her for a Stuart Erwin comedy, *Pigskin Parade*. The film, about a small-time Texas football team that is invited to play Yale, is remembered today solely for its cast: Erwin, Judy (who played Stu's kid sister, Sairy), Patsy Kelly, Jack Haley, Betty Grable, Tony Martin, Grady Sutton, and Elisha Cook, Jr.

Fox gave her three songs to do in the picture. The music made working on the film an enjoyable experience for Judy, but it failed to make the picture a smash at the box office. The reviews were hardly raves, but the *New York Times* called Judy a newcomer "about whom the West Coast has been enthusing as a vocal find." The newspaper went on to say, "She's cute, not too pretty, but a pleasingly fetching personality, who certainly knows how to sell a pop."

Adela Rogers St. Johns later remembered that the primary problem with Judy's appearance at this stage in her life was her weight. "The first time I ever saw her, she was prancing . . . this time around a foot-

Judy inspects a tune to be used in her first feature picture, *Pigskin Parade*. With her are costar Tony Martin (left), songwriter Sidney D. Mitchell, and costar Jack Haley.

ball field, and I wasn't sure she was a drum majorette or the left guard. As far as I could see she was perfectly square. Then I heard her singing a fight-on song in a voice that *literally* sent shivers up and down my spine."

Because Judy's weight problem also concerned her mentors at MGM, Mayer put her on a strict diet of chicken broth, chicken broth, and more chicken broth.

"The studio began grooming me," Judy recalled later. "I learned how to walk, how to carry myself better. I got to know the other players on the lot. And I began to work with Mrs. Rose Carter, who was engaged by the studio as my private tutor."

In January 1937, three important events took place: on January 5, Judy made a well-received guest appearance on the second broadcast of Jack Oakie's new CBS radio series, *Jack Oakie's College*. So impressed were the producers that they invited her back for the program of February 23.

At MGM, producer Jack Cummings was beginning to piece together plans for his latest Eleanor Powell picture, *Broadway Melody of 1937*. Having missed using Judy in both *Born to Dance* and *Broadway Melody of 1936*, Cummings hoped to include her services this time around.

Louis B. Mayer, Cummings' uncle, had a more urgent assignment: the studio's most popular male star, Clark Gable, was having a birthday February

Judy appears with comedian Jack Oakie on his popular radio series in 1937.

1, and Mayer wanted to surprise him with a special party. He asked studio songwriter Arthur Freed and Roger Edens to plan the musical entertainment. Edens, aware of Judy's tentative status at the studio, thought immediately of using her.

Judy was ecstatic. She adored Gable and knew immediately what she wanted to sing—a sophisticated better-days-are-coming song from 1932 that Edens had arranged for Ethel Merman to use in a nightclub act. "I wanted to do 'Drums in My Heart,' " Judy recalled later, "but Roger said no. Simple songs were best for children. He wrote something else for me, and he was right. The people liked it, and it started me on my real screen career."

The "something else" that Edens came up with was a rewrite of a monologue he had written a few months earlier for Carmel Myers to perform on Rudy Vallee's radio show. In the new version, Judy would be a young girl writing a fan letter to her favorite movie star. The sequence would end with Judy belting the lyrics to a song her father had taught her, "You Made Me Love You."

Seeking a title, Edens decided to have a little inside fun with Gable. A young Englishwoman had been bombarding the studio recently with letters, claiming that Clark was the father of her child. Each of the letters began the same way—"Dear Mr. Gable."

The party was held on the set of *Parnell,* a film Gable was shooting with Myrna Loy. A big cake was rolled out and someone presented him with a paper crown, in honor of his title as "king of the movies." As the crown was being tied on with a ribbon, Gable quipped, "Put the ribbon over my ears to keep them down." Judy, sitting on a little wooden box and staring at the photograph of the birthday boy, began to sing . . . "Dear Mr. Gable, I am writing this to you," and suddenly everyone's ears perked up to listen. At the end of the song, Gable gave her a big hug. She had been sensational!

Judy repeated her song a few weeks later for an MGM exhibitors' gathering; when that performance proved as successful as the first, Mayer and Cummings agreed to put both Judy and the song into *Broadway Melody of 1937.* She portrayed the teenage daughter of Sophie Tucker, the proprietress of a theatrical boardinghouse.

On February 23, as the movie started production,

Dear Mr. Gable: Judy sings for the "King" at a party for Clark Gable's thirty-sixth birthday in 1937.

Judy returned to *Jack Oakie's College* and sang her "letter to Clark Gable" for all the country to hear. The song was so popular that she kept it in her repertoire until the day Gable died.

Broadway Melody of 1937 (later retitled *Broadway Melody of 1938*) starred Eleanor Powell, Robert Taylor, Binnie Barnes, and Buddy Ebsen, who danced with Judy in the film's finale.

Still nervous about Judy's chubbiness, Metro reportedly introduced her to benzedrine and other diet pills during the production of this musical. She would have problems with drugs for the rest of her life.

MGM gave Judy the full "promising newcomer" treatment. Publicity layouts were planned for major magazines, complete with dazzling photographs and often fictionalized biographical information. Magazines loved to feature pictures of Hollywood stars celebrating the holidays, and photos were taken of Judy with Halloween pumpkins, Thanksgiving turkeys, Christmas sleighs, and New Year's hats. Every possible effort was made to put her name before the public.

Judy made a third guest appearance with Jack Oakie on March 9, after which the comedian asked her to become a regular on his show. Metro thought the added exposure a fine idea; for thirteen weeks, between March 30 and June 22, Judy made the trek between MGM and CBS Radio's KNX facilities in Hollywood.

Radio adaptations of new movies were quite in vogue during the 1930s and 1940s. On July 16, as production was finishing on *Broadway Melody of 1938*, much of the cast, including Judy, trooped over to CBS to do a shortened version for *Hollywood Hotel*.

In August, Judy signed a long-term contract with Decca Records. She now had a foothold in all three of the major media of the day. At last Judy Garland was making a name for herself.

Judy's home life was going through a series of changes and adjustments. She and Ethel had moved to a two-story home in Hollywood. Virginia no longer lived with them. Like Mary Jane, Virginia had married a musician, Bobby Sherwood, and she was now expecting a child.

Judy, about to make her MGM debut, reads from her home-town paper.

Broadway Melody of 1938 opened to fine reviews. Harrison Carroll wrote: "It is thirteen-year-old Judy Garland with her singing who really walks away with the picture. Here is not only a complete artist, but a personality that takes you by storm. Her spirited rendition of 'Everybody Sing,' and her handling of pathos in 'Dear Mr. Gable' were the high spots in the picture for me."

MGM assigned Judy to two new pictures shooting back-to-back that fall. *Thoroughbreds Don't Cry* was Judy's first appearance with her classmate and good friend Mickey Rooney. Also in the cast were Sophie Tucker, C. Aubrey Smith, and Ronald Sinclair. Sophie was again cast as the owner of a boardinghouse, a lodging for young jockeys. Mickey played a young rider who has never lost a race, Sinclair an English boy whose grandfather (Smith) brings his horse to the United States.

Judy, who played Sophie's live-in niece, said that it was Mickey who helped her through this first real acting assignment. "I'd been in vaudeville for several years with my family, but never had I been asked to read a line. I was frightened to death until Mickey, the veteran, put his arm around me and said, 'Honey, you've got to believe in what you're saying and doing— that's the whole secret of acting. And when you sing, make like you mean it and live the part.' "

The second movie was originally titled *The Ugly Duckling*, with Judy cast in the title role. It started filming as soon as *Thoroughbreds* finished, but it had been renamed *Everybody Sing* to capitalize on the success of Judy's song from *Broadway Melody*. Judy's character in the film was that of a plain Jane who at one point in the story is referred to as "my ugly duckling daughter." Billie Burke and Reginald Owen were theatre folk. Judy played their daughter, who gets expelled from a snooty upper-crust girls' school for singing Mendelssohn to a swingtime beat.

The first week of November, Judy took time out from her feature work to appear in MGM's *1937 Christmas Trailer*, a ten-minute film to be run in theatres during the holidays. Holding a candle and standing before a stained-glass window, Judy sang "Silent Night."

That month Judy became a regular on Maxwell House Coffee's *Good News of 1938*, the first network radio series to be produced in association with a

The big studios loved to have their new stars posing in publicity shots tied in with the holidays.

The cast of *Broadway Melody of 1938* rehearse the radio version at CBS. Left to right: Charles I. Gorin, Judy, Billy Gilbert, George Murphy, Sophie Tucker, Eleanor Powell, Buddy Ebsen, Harriet Parsons (hostess), Robert Taylor, and Frances Langford.

BELOW: One of the first ads for Judy was placed in *Variety*.

major Hollywood studio. MGM made every star on the lot ("except Garbo") available for the NBC broadcasts. Judy was featured on the premiere, November 4, 1937, along with Jeanette MacDonald, Sophie Tucker, and Eva Tanguay, and appeared eleven more times before the season ended in May.

While Judy was shuttling back and forth between her film assignments and radio broadcasts, songwriter Arthur Freed, who wanted to start a new career as a film producer, asked Louis B. Mayer for permission to seek out a musical property that would allow him to spotlight "the young Garland girl," for whom Freed saw a great future. Mayer agreed; by February 1938, as *Everybody Sing* was being released to the theatres, Freed had found his vehicle. On February 24, *Variety* carried the news that MGM was purchasing the screen rights to L. Frank Baum's *The Wizard of Oz* and that Judy would be cast as Dorothy.

Judy was out of town the day the story broke: she had been booked for a six-week nationwide tour, appearing at theatres showing *Everybody Sing*. The official premiere was in Miami Beach, with stops in Pittsburgh, New York City, Chicago, and Columbus, Ohio—where she was named the "Sweetheart of Sigma Chi."

In Manhattan, Judy was thrilled to see her name in huge letters on the Times Square marquee of the Loews State Theatre.

Everybody Sing was warmly received. *Film Weekly* commented:

It's a little early to predict but here's a prophecy for 1938!

JUDY GARLAND

STARDOM !

16

Judy Garland is an extremely clever little comedienne. She proves it in a delightful duet with Fanny Brice, and anyone who can stand up to Miss Brice at her own comedy game is very good indeed. Also, Judy's is the number which lifts the picture into the "excellent" class. Her burlesque of "Swing Low, Sweet Chariot," complete with blacked face and "Uncle Tom's Cabin" curls, is as good as anything I have seen in my recent film going.

Judy returned to MGM in April to start work not on *The Wizard of Oz*, which was scheduled to go into production in July, but on the fourth installment in Mickey Rooney's *Andy Hardy* series—*Love Finds Andy Hardy*. One of the biggest-grossing films of the year, *Love Finds Andy Hardy* proved pure magic. Mickey had emerged as a major star, and the addition of Judy to the series as a visiting neighbor was magic. The love interest was played by another budding young talent, Lana Turner, who had just signed a contract with MGM.

Despite her success, Judy was still overly concerned about her appearance, especially in the com-

ABOVE: Judy swings Mendelssohn and causes havoc in *Everybody Sing*.

Judy works with Bronislaw Kaper, Walter Jurmann, and Gus Kahn on the songs from *Everybody Sing*.

pany of such beautiful costars as Lana Turner and Ann Rutherford. Maxine Marx, Chico's daughter, remembers bumping into Judy one day that spring in the ladies' room at the studio. Judy had been crying.

"What's the matter?" Maxine asked.

"I'm so ugly!" Judy replied.

"You are *not!*"

"Yes, I am. Look at Lana and Annie."

"But they have none of your talent," Maxine tried to explain. "You're the one who has it all."

"Who cares?" Judy said dejectedly.

Judy was about to become an aunt. Virginia's first child was due any day. As it turned out, nearly the whole family wound up in the hospital together. On May 24, Judy was on her way home from work when the automobile in which she was riding was hit broadside by another car. Judy was rushed to Cedars of Lebanon Hospital with three broken ribs and multiple bruises. A day or two later, a nurse escorted Judy in a wheelchair to the nursery window, where, for the first time, she saw Judy Gail Sherwood, nicknamed "Judalein" ("little Judy").

Judy's career was on a roll. Everyone suddenly knew who she was, and MGM was delighted to give her more and more work. Sixteen days after *Love Finds Andy Hardy* wrapped production, the studio assigned her to *Listen, Darling,* a lightweight, down-home musical with a heavyweight cast. *Wizard,* trying to overcome script problems, had been postponed

until October. Freddie Bartholomew, Mary Astor, Walter Pidgeon, Alan Hale, Charley Grapewin, and Gene Lockhart joined Judy in *Listen, Darling,* the story of two children who attempt to keep their mother from marrying solely for financial security. The plot was predictable—but so were Judy's fine songs. She did "Zing! Went the Strings of My Heart," "On the Bumpy Road to Love," and "Ten Pins in the Sky," a tune she liked well enough to record that summer for Decca.

Costar Mary Astor remembered this as a joyous time for Judy: "Working with Judy was sheer joy. She was young and vital and got the giggles regularly. You couldn't get annoyed, because she couldn't help it—it was no act."

Things at home were more somber. Mary Jane's marriage to Lee Kahn had ended in divorce, and worse, Ethel had started to date a man named Will Gilmore, a widower and former neighbor from Lancaster. Judy, who revered the memory of her father, considered this sacrilege.

Judy cheered herself with plans to build a new home on Stone Canyon Road in West Los Angeles. She wanted the house to be white and sprawling, with plenty of trees and flowers, a swimming pool, and also a tennis court where she could entertain Mickey and the gang from the studio. The house would be big enough for Ethel to share, but Judy, now sixteen years old, would have her own private suite and entrances.

Judy is interviewed by Sam Park, a WIOD announcer, as she arrives in Miami for the premiere of *Everybody Sing.*

Judy as Betsy Booth, Andy Hardy's neighbor in *Love Finds Andy Hardy.*

Listen, Darling rushed into theatres that fall, receiving positive, if unenthusiastic, reviews. The *New York Times* found it to be a "natural, pleasant little film," calling Judy "a charming little miss" with "a fresh young voice." Another publication warned, however, that while "Judy is sweet and she can sing prettily . . . these, too, too homey stories aren't her best medium. She's a lot better when she's bouncing around, singing a little hot-cha, not moping the better share of the time about mama's troubles. In fact, Judy is getting to the age when something must be done about her. She is pretty chubby and bids fair to grow chubbier. If her contract holders want to make some money out of her, they'd best be looking to her diet."

The studio doctors were prescribing more and more benzedrine to help keep her weight off; and the studio had all kinds of new projects waiting in the wings for her.

Ethel started to worry about the heavy work schedule Judy had taken on. Her daughter seemed so *nervous* lately. "I'd like her to be a little more carefree and not assume so much responsibility," she told one reporter. "I'd like her to enjoy the things that other girls do."

OVERLEAF: Betsy Booth dons glamour for her last visit with the Hardys in *Life Begins for Andy Hardy.*

19

That little girl's vocal chords are heart strings.
MERVYN LEROY

he *Wizard of Oz,* one of the most elaborate in-studio motion pictures ever conceived, went into production at MGM on October 13, 1938. The plot concerned a young farm girl, Dorothy Gale, who is struck on the head during a Kansas tornado and dreams she goes "over the rainbow" to the colorful land of Oz.

Judy, of course, was cast as Dorothy, although various studio chieftains had someone else in mind for that role. As Mervyn LeRoy, who was brought in to produce the picture, recalled, "Some of the producers at Metro wanted Shirley Temple, but I always wanted Judy Garland. On account of her voice. On account of her personality. She *looked* more like Dorothy than Shirley did. I insisted we had to make a test of her, and she was sensational."

Also in the cast were Ray Bolger, Bert Lahr, Frank Morgan, Charley Grapewin, Clara Blandick, Billie Burke, and Margaret Hamilton. Buddy Ebsen, Judy's dance partner from *Broadway Melody,* started the movie, but was replaced after two weeks by Jack Haley.

The music for the film was by Harold Arlen, the lyrics by E. Y. Harburg, the musical adaptation by Herbert Stothart. The score included the song that would forever after be Judy's theme song, "Over the Rainbow."

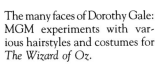

The many faces of Dorothy Gale: MGM experiments with various hairstyles and costumes for *The Wizard of Oz*.

Judy, like countless other girls, fell in love with musician Artie Shaw, partying here at the Brown Derby.

Arthur Freed, who had hoped to produce *Wizard* himself, allowed Mayer to give the extremely complicated picture to the more experienced LeRoy, with the proviso that Freed be retained as Mervyn's assistant.

Freed, however, was never one to devote all his energies to just one project, and he started to diversify his interests even before *Wizard* began shooting. On October 7, he bought rights to Rodgers and Hart's Broadway hit *Babes in Arms*, with Judy and Mickey Rooney in mind for the leads. To ensure that this one would not be taken away from him, he promptly negotiated his own new contract with the studio. Producer Arthur Freed had arrived.

Because of the complicated production schedule for *The Wizard of Oz*, Judy was forced to cut back drastically on her radio appearances. On September 8, she appeared on NBC's *Good News* program to promote *Love Finds Andy Hardy* and returned October 20 to plug *Listen, Darling*, but her almost-weekly appearances on the show were over. She did manage to find time to appear on an NBC program December 14 heralding the National Rededication Movement, and on January 8, 1939, she helped launch the new *Screen Guild Theatre* series on CBS.

On January 22, Judy joined Mickey Rooney and

a dozen other stars on Eddie Cantor's *Council of Stars* broadcast for the March of Dimes. In March, and again in May, Judy visited Bob Hope's new *Pepsodent Show*. Finally, on June 29, she returned to *Good News* to promote *The Wizard of Oz*.

Judy was now officially considered a star. In November 1938, MGM announced her new status. To solemnize the occasion it gave her a new dressing room decorated in a red, white, and blue nautical motif, complete with anchors and ship's lamps on the wall. "Judy loves boats and the sea," a family friend explained at the time, "but she has never been on a boat for any length of time. She says her dressing room is the next-best thing."

Although MGM's publicity department continually referred to their new star as a precocious fourteen year old, Judy was in fact sixteen and, like most teenagers, beginning to notice the opposite sex. Jazz musician Artie Shaw, whom she had met in New York the previous spring, was one of her first major crushes.

The Wizard of Oz, in production for over five months, finally wrapped on March 16, 1939. MGM rewarded Judy for a job well done with a holiday in New York. Ethel accompanied her, and they were greeted at the train by a phalanx of reporters and photographers. The Garlands spent much of their time seeing the season's latest Broadway shows. *One for the Money,* featuring a young dancer named Gene Kelly, was a particular favorite.

Never able to get away from work, Judy paid a

Judy and Mickey Rooney relax at Hollywood Park, 1939.

visit to CBS Radio's New York studios April 6 for a guest appearance with Andre Kostelanetz and his orchestra. The forty-five-minute weekly series was called, fittingly, *Tune Up Time.*

Returning to Hollywood, Judy started rehearsals on Arthur Freed's new production of *Babes in Arms.* Written by Jack McGowan and Kay Van Riper, the script remained rather faithful to the original Broadway production. Judy and Mickey were offsprings of down-on-their-luck theatrical parents determined to inject new life into Mom and Pop's old-hat routines.

Legendary director Busby Berkeley started shooting *Babes* on May 12 and finished it eight weeks later with virtually no problems. Cast along with Judy and Mickey were June Preisser, Margaret Hamilton, Charles Winninger, Guy Kibbee, Grace Hayes, Betty Jaynes, Douglas McPhail, Rand Brooks, Leni Lynn, and John Sheffield (soon to be "Boy" in MGM's *Tarzan* series).

Judy celebrated her seventeenth birthday during the production of *Babes in Arms,* and was given her first automobile—an oxblood-red Cadillac sedan.

Judy's Decca records continued to sell; in July she recorded six new songs.

The world premiere of *The Wizard of Oz* at Grauman's Chinese Theatre on August 15, 1939, was one of the great Hollywood events of its time. The rite was repeated two days later at the Capitol Theatre in New York, where the film was accompanied by live stage appearances by Judy and Mickey Rooney. Opening day broke the house record. As the *Hollywood Reporter* explained, "The lines started to form at 5:30 in the morning and when the box office opened at eight there were 15,000 four abreast lined up around the corner almost to Eighth Avenue."

Biographer Gerold Frank in his book, *Judy,* recalls that by this trip Judy had grown taller than Mickey, and so while they were on stage together:

> . . . she would appear surreptitiously to push one shoe off with the toe of her foot, do the same with the other foot, and then, in her stocking feet the same height as Mickey, go into her act with him. On one occasion she collapsed backstage just when she was about to go on: she simply slumped and fainted. Whether it was exhaustion or a sudden drop in blood sugar (she virtually lived on Coca-Colas when she could), she was unable

Judy and Mickey join Jack Haley in New York for the premiere of *The Wizard of Oz* in 1939.

to go on. Mickey covered for her, ad-libbing and clowning cleverly, and in a little while Judy, who had been given immediate medical attention backstage, had revived. Before reaching New York she and Mickey had undergone the grueling ordeal of "breaking in" their act by rushing through personal appearances in three cities—Washington, New Haven, and Hartford—and from the moment they arrived in New York they had to cope with welcoming committees . . . luncheons and constant interviews. Judy's collapse was her first from overwork—and the forerunner of many more.

Judy later recalled the special evening she, Ethel, and Mickey spent at the Rainbow Room, high above Rockefeller Center. "We wanted to know how it felt to dance on top of the world!"

That week Fred Waring invited Judy to appear on his radio program. "Of course, I accepted, thinking he just wanted me to say 'hello.' Do you know what he did? He had his entire program dedicated to *me*! And his theme song for the evening was 'Over the Rainbow.' So I sang all the songs from *The Wizard of Oz* for him, and a good time was had by all—most especially by me!"

The Wizard of Oz received mostly sensational reviews. The *New York Times* called it "a delightful piece of wonder-working," and the *New York Post* added that "Miss Garland makes a delightful Dorothy." The *New York Daily News* elaborated, "She is as clever a little actress as she is a singer and her special style of vocalizing is ideally adapted to the music of the picture."

The music from *The Wizard of Oz* proved particularly popular. On September 28, Judy recorded "Over the Rainbow" and "The Jitterbug" (which had been cut from the picture after the first preview) for Decca.

The 1939–1940 radio season was starting. On September 24, Judy joined Mickey Rooney, Cary Grant, and Ann Sothern in the fall premiere of *Screen Guild Theatre*. Bob Hope, pleased with Judy's two appearances on his show the previous spring, invited her to be a regular cast member this season. Judy's role was both resident singer and heckler, with most of her jibes pointed at the host himself. Hope had an opportunity to even the score a few weeks later when Judy's optometrist prescribed glasses. She chose a fashionable pair with big horn-rimmed frames, but Bob kidded her about them both in rehearsals and on the air.

On October 13, Judy was invited to press her foot and hand prints into the cement of the forecourt at Grauman's Chinese Theatre, a ritual accorded only to Hollywood's recognized royalty. Premiering there that evening was *Babes in Arms*, one of the biggest money-makers of the year.

More Decca recordings followed, and MGM started

ABOVE: Judy puts her footprints in the forecourt at Grauman's Chinese Theatre in Hollywood, 1939.

BELOW: Crowds form early for Judy and Mickey's personal appearances at New York's Capitol Theatre in 1939.

Betsy Booth comes to Andy's rescue again in *Andy Hardy Meets Debutante*.

discussing plans for a new picture. Arthur Freed had already lined up a remake of a collegiate musical comedy, *Good News*, to be his next "kid picture" and was close to closing a deal with George M. Cohan for *Little Nellie Kelly*. Freed knew both would be excellent for Judy, but neither project was ready to go, so to fill the gap MGM suggested another installment in the life of Andy Hardy.

Ethel was making a few plans of her own. Feeling the need for marital stability and companionship, she and Will Gilmore announced their intentions to get married. None of the Garland girls was particularly fond of Gilmore, but they might have warmed up to the idea of a stepfather had Ethel not insisted on doing things her own way. On November 17, her birthday—and the fourth anniversary of Frank Gumm's death—she and Gilmore impetuously eloped. "That was the most awful thing that ever happened," Judy confessed. "My mother marrying that awful man the same day that my daddy died."

Andy Hardy Meets Debutante was the ninth in MGM's Hardy series (Mickey had done four of the films in the eighteen months since *Love Finds Andy Hardy* wrapped). Clearly not a big picture in the same league as *Wizard* or *Babes*, *Debutante* was designed to keep the Garland-Rooney team working and to satisfy ticket buyers' unquenchable thirst for

more visits with the Hardy family. So popular were the Hardys that MGM also prepared a special ten-minute radio disc, distributed to stations around the country, in which Andy, his mother, father, and sister wished everyone a Merry Christmas, 1939, and a prosperous and peaceful New Year. Spliced into

Judy joins boss Louis B. Mayer in welcoming singer Tony Martin to MGM.

26

Judy gets a kiss on the cheek from Mickey after winning a special Oscar for her performance in *The Wizard of Oz.*

the program was Judy's performance of "Silent Night," lifted from the 1937 Christmas trailer the studio had issued two years earlier.

In February, Artie Shaw, for whom Judy still cared a great deal, eloped with Lana Turner. Judy was shattered by the news, now more convinced than ever that beauty was more important to a man than talent. She reported as scheduled the next night to NBC for a rehearsal of *The Bob Hope Show.* Judy's eyes were still red and puffy, so David Rose, the twenty-nine-year-old composer-arranger working across the hall on the Tony Martin show, attempted to comfort her. He offered her a slice of homemade chocolate cake (denied by MGM's strict diets), and that night they went out together. Before long, she had forgotten all about the elusive Mr. Shaw.

On February 29, the Academy of Motion Picture Arts and Sciences presented Judy with a special "juvenile" Oscar for her performance in *The Wizard of*

Oz. It was a special evening made even more special because the Academy had chosen Mickey Rooney to present the award to her. Garland accepted her Oscar to a standing ovation and then obliged the audience with a rendition of "Over the Rainbow"— which also won an award that night for Best Song of the Year.

Judy later described that night as "the most sensational moment of my career. . . . The lump in my throat was so big when I sang 'Over the Rainbow' that I sounded more like Flip the Frog than the most excited girl in all Hollywood. And I'll never forget how Mickey came to my rescue, for I was so nervous I thought I'd faint. He practically held me up through the second chorus."

A week after the awards banquet, Judy received her first real taste of the dark side of stardom. Two young men tried to kidnap her. Robert Wilson, nineteen, of Buffalo, New York, drifted into Los Angeles, where he met fellow drifter Frank Foster. "Hang around with me," Foster promised, "and you'll be rolling in dough—but you've gotta keep your mouth shut!" Foster's plan was to kidnap Judy from her home in Bel Air, drive into the mountains, and hold her for $50,000 ransom.

Judy offers refreshment to police detectives dispatched to protect her against suspected kidnappers in 1940.

At the last minute Wilson panicked and called the local police. Officers were immediately dispatched to Judy's home, where she was entertaining a group of friends. They locked the doors, turned off the lights and waited . . . but Foster never showed. Wilson's call was traced to a Santa Monica telephone, and he was soon arrested.

Judy continued to record for Decca, and Arthur Freed proceeded with plans for *Good News.* L. B. Mayer, however, had noted the new surge of patriotism that was sweeping the country—war had already broken out in Europe—and he suggested that Freed set aside his college musical and make *Strike Up the Band* instead. "It sounds so patriotic!" he said.

Judy and Mickey jump for joy to celebrate their latest success in Strike Up the Band.

Judy poses with one of the first Judy Garland look-alike dolls issued at Christmastime, 1940.

Freed agreed but threw out the book of the original 1930 Broadway show and asked writers Fred Finklehoffe and John Marks, Jr., to come up with a new story—one suitable for Mickey and Judy and not too dissimilar to the plots used so successfully in the past. The new story, which sounded something like "Babes in Arms Meets Andy Hardy," concerned a high school drummer (Mickey) who hopes to become a bandleader like his idol, Paul Whiteman (who played himself in the picture). Judy, the girl singer in the band, helps him raise $200 to go to Chicago to participate in a big band contest, but their plans are thwarted when a friend becomes ill and their newly acquired money has to go to pay the medical expenses. Not to worry—Paul Whiteman comes to town, and Mick's group gets to audition after all.

Busby Berkeley directed, and the cast included June Preisser, Ann Shoemaker, Larry Nunn, Francis Peirlot, Virginia Brissac, Enid Bonnett, and Helen Jerome Nelson.

During the production of *Strike Up the Band,* a new face was added to what was becoming known around town as "the Freed Unit." Broadway designer-director Vincente Minnelli had come aboard to "learn the business" and make suggestions here and there until he felt comfortable with the film medium.

In his autobiography, *I Remember It Well*, Minnelli recalled the afternoon he met Judy: " 'Glad to meet you,' she bubbled cheerfully. I was attracted to her open manner, as only a man who has been reserved all his life can be."

Judy celebrated her eighteenth birthday at the home of Louis B. Mayer, and a couple of weeks later, on June 26, she was graduated from University High School.

Judy's next picture, *Little Nellie Kelly*, directed by Norman Taurog, went into production while *Strike Up the Band* was still shooting. In this new film, Garland got her first opportunity to play an adult—two of them: an immigrant mother who dies in childbirth and the grownup child. George Murphy was cast as Judy's husband/father and Charles Winninger as Nellie's maternal grandfather.

"I was so nervous about this role!" Judy said later. "I never will forget the day I had to do my first real love scene. It was with George Murphy, and I felt so silly, I couldn't look him in the eye. I felt that I had to apologize to everyone on the set by saying, 'Unaccustomed as I am to public love scenes . . .' "

During the production of the picture, MGM canceled the two years remaining on Judy's 1935 contract and offered her an all new seven-year pact, starting at $2000 per week! It was a wise investment: *Andy Hardy Meets Debutante* had opened that summer to great success, and the studio had every reason to believe *Strike Up the Band* would do likewise. When the picture opened in New York on September 30, the *Times* wrote, "Roll out the red carpet, folks . . . this show has everything—music, laughter, tears . . . *Strike Up the Band* is spanking good entertainment."

The one thing Judy's new contract forbade was weekly radio exposure. She could no longer be a "regular" on a series as she had with Bob Hope and Jack Oakie. Occasional guest appearances, however, were still encouraged, and Judy's radio agenda that fall included adaptations of both *Strike Up the Band*

and *Little Nellie Kelly*, a Christmas Eve visit with Hope, a New Year's Day *Bundles for Britain* broadcast, and a visit with Edgar Bergen and Charlie McCarthy on *The Chase and Sanborn Hour*.

During the first week in October, Judy underwent an operation common to children but often frightening for most singers: she had her tonsils removed. She noticed a change when she sang, for the better. "My throat always felt tight before," she told her doctors. "Now it seems to open up."

"Gorgeously vulgar, blindingly all-star, and irresistibly supercolossal" were among the adjectives heaped on Judy's next MGM assignment—producer Pan Berman's *Ziegfeld Girl*—and these were just the kind of words Ziggy would have been proud to hear.

Judy in the colorful "Minnie from Trinidad" number in *Ziegfeld Girl*, costume by Adrian (1941).

Judy's relationship with her mother, Ethel, ran from hot to cold, but it was always loving (1941).

The film was one of the studio's biggest hits of 1941.

Appearing with Judy in this bonanza were James Stewart, Hedy Lamarr, Lana Turner, Tony Martin, Jackie Cooper, Ian Hunter, Charles Winninger, Edward Everett Horton, Dan Dailey, Fay Holden, Eve Arden, and Al Shean.

The picture's main plot involved three girls sponsored by Florenz Ziegfeld. Judy was again typecast as a vaudevillian, an entertainer who makes it to the top through talent and hard work. Lamarr played an entertainer who gives up her career to please her husband, and Turner, who stole the picture, was the promising young hopeful who finds unhappiness at the bottom of a bottle.

Judy was a nervous wreck throughout much of the picture. All her old fears about being "a thorn between two roses" returned, and even having such old pals as Jackie Cooper, whom she once dated, on the set did not help.

That winter her personal life was dominated by her continuing relationship with musician David Rose. What had started as a casual relationship had evolved into a serious love affair. The situation was complicated not only because David was twelve years older than Judy but also because he was still waiting for a divorce from his first wife, Martha Raye.

Professionally, Judy and David were wonderful together. He would visit her home in Bel Air and work out new arrangements for her Decca records; she would stimulate his interest in certain pieces of music he had not previously considered. David also encouraged Judy to express herself with pen and paper, and she turned out a portfolio of nine poems, *Thoughts and Poems by Judy Garland,* copies of which she gave as gifts.

Ethel was not crazy about her daughter's dating a married man and asked friends to discourage Judy from continuing the relationship. Instead, her resistance only strengthened it.

In December, Judy showed David a story she had written, a sketch about a young girl in love with an older man. David immediately saw merit in the work, suggested that it be adapted for radio, and started working out musical arrangements to accompany the story. A few weeks later, on January 26, Judy's sketch, "Love's New Sweet Song," dramatized by True Boardman, aired on CBS's *Silver Theatre.* Judy starred in the program, along with William McCullom and Elliot Lewis.

On February 22, David escorted Judy to the annual Oscars, a night remembered by the Academy as the first award ceremony to be addressed by the president of the United States. Franklin D. Roosevelt spoke to the audience via radio, after which Judy was asked to sing "America."

Judy and David were seen in many night spots that spring, but, in deference both to the studio and her mother, Judy agreed to downplay the romance for the press and to be seen in public with other men. Among her escorts were Peter Lind Hayes, Dan Dailey, and Robert Stack.

Stack recalled, "Ida Mae Coverman [sic] was second in command under Louis B. Mayer at MGM. She was also a friend of mother and thought it would be 'darling' if Judy and I had a romance.

" 'They make such a cute couple,' she said. As in every such case, nothing developed. Judy was in love at various times with Artie Shaw, David Rose, and other musical types, while I was researching the list of contract girls. But we were always great chums."

Finally, in May, David received his divorce, and Judy and Rose decided to marry. The announcement was made at a cocktail party Judy held at her Bel Air home. Guests included Joan Crawford, Jimmy Stewart, George Murphy, Eleanor Powell, Lana Turner, Tony Martin, Freddie Bartholomew, Jane Withers, and Bob Sterling. The event, ostensibly to celebrate both Judy and David's birthdays, was held outside on the tennis court, which Judy had decorated with beautiful tables and huge parasols. David gave Judy a ruby cocktail ring, and she gave him a pair of cufflinks she had designed. One link bore the inscription YOU ME; the other was engraved with a measure of music and the word US. To top off the day, David presented her with a 3½-carat square-cut diamond ring, with emerald baguettes on each side—an engagement present worth $2000. The couple planned to marry in the fall.

Judy sings "America" during the thirteenth annual Academy Awards presentation in 1941.

David Rose catches a pie in the face from Judy when they cavort at Milton Berle's Mack Sennett bathing party. Watching in the background are Buster Keaton and Ann Miller (1941).

Joan Crawford hugs Judy at Judy's engagement party to David Rose.

MGM, ecstatic over the success of *Ziegfeld Girl*, had no major musical in the works to follow. Instead, they asked Judy to make one last visit to the mythical town of Carvel and the *Andy Hardy* series. Installment number eleven, *Life Begins for Andy Hardy*, found Andy growing into young adulthood and wandering off to New York before deciding on how to spend his future. Betsy Booth (Judy) accompanies and watches over him, until he returns to Carvel, ready to follow his father's suggestions of a college education.

Judy's next project, *Babes on Broadway*, was something of a followup to *Babes in Arms* and *Strike Up the Band*, reuniting her with Freed, Berkeley, and, of course, costar Rooney.

Judy and Mickey were again cast as talented youngsters struggling for success. This time they were

trying to make it big on the Great White Way. Eventually discouraged, they decide that the only way to win recognition is to put on a show of their own. They stage a benefit for orphans, and lo and behold, they end up stars on Broadway!

Joining Mickey and Judy this time were Fay Bainter, Virginia Weidler, Ray McDonald, Richard Quine, Donald Meek, Alexander Woollcott, and James Gleason. Making her motion picture debut in an unbilled appearance was four-year-old Margaret O'Brien.

Production got under way on July 14, but two weeks later Judy disappeared—she and David Rose had run off, with Ethel and Will Gilmore in tow, to Las Vegas to get married. The morning of July 28 Arthur Freed received a telegram: "I am so very happy. Dave and I were married this AM. Give me a little time and I will be back and finish the picture with one take on each scene. Love, Judy."

Of course, MGM had never really approved of Judy's getting married in the first place. L. B. Mayer knew that marriage to anyone would alter the "sweet young teenager" image that the studio had so carefully cultivated for Judy. Now that the deed was done, the studio would have to live with it—but on its own terms. A honeymoon was out of the question, Metro answered back; *Babes on Broadway* cannot be delayed.

Judy and David returned to Los Angeles the very next day, and Mrs. Rose, minus some of the respect she had once had for her employers, finished her film on schedule. She flatly refused, however, to film

Judy and Mickey confer with musical director Georgie Stoll and director Busby Berkeley for their new film, *Babes on Broadway.*

Judy relaxes at home on her days off in 1938.

her scenes without her wedding ring. A studio craftsman saved the day when he came up with a special setting that could be clipped onto Judy's gold band, disguising it to look like an ordinary ring.

And so it was that Judy started life as Mrs. David Rose. She had so many hopes for the future—she saw herself as wife, mother, and Hollywood hostess. Never did she consider that things in real life do not always turn out as happily as they do in the movies.

OVERLEAF: Portrait by John Engstead.

She believed every word, and her sincerity made believers of us all. Her kind of talent comes along once in a generation.

VINCENTE MINNELLI

"Judy Garland's biggest fault," announced a 1941 movie magazine, "is allowing herself to be imposed upon. She can't say no . . . to photographers, to publicists, to anyone. Judy often gives up her day off, cancels whatever plans she may have had for herself, and with no complaining. . . ."

Judy had indeed become something of a workaholic, but, once married, she also channeled as much of her energies as possible toward establishing a home for herself and David. The newlyweds had determined early on that they could not live with Ethel and Will Gilmore in the house Judy owned in Bel Air, and Judy had no real desire to live in David's small home in the San Fernando Valley. Instead, they moved into a Hollywood-style mansion, the former home of Jean Harlow.

The house, redecorated by an interim owner, came decorated in a pseudo-eighteenth-century motif, complete with copies of French antiques, satins, and brocades. What reportedly sold David on the house, however, was not the interior, but rather the back yard: it was spacious and flat. David's hobby was miniature railroads, and at his home in the valley he had laid nearly 780 feet of track; for a wedding present, Judy had given him a fine new depot. The new house accommodated David's trains nicely, and the whole setup was christened "The Gar-Rose Railway."

Almost from the beginning, the marriage suffered from the two-career syndrome. Judy, despite her good intentions, did not have time for the demands of a home and husband—not at the rate MGM was using her. David's musical chores often kept him busy at night; her film work demanded she be at the studio all day. It was not an easy situation.

To whet the public's appetite for *Babes on Broadway*, Judy and Mickey recreated their earlier hit, *Babes in Arms*, on CBS Radio's *Screen Guild Theatre* November 9. A week later, they teamed up again for a *Lux Radio Theatre* adaptation of the George S. Kaufman–Marc Connelly comedy, "Merton of the Movies."

The Motion Picture Industry's annual Community Chest Drive got under way November 3, and at noon, Louis B. Mayer inaugurated the 1941 drive with a speech on radio station KFWB. Judy sang the new Chest theme song, "Share a Little." A second such broadcast was heard December 15 from the Biltmore Bowl. This time Judy introduced a new song by Jerome Kern, "Abe Lincoln Had Only One Country," accompanied by Leon Leonard's KFWB orchestra.

In the six weeks that lapsed between these two broadcasts, a lot happened to Judy, and to the country. On Sunday, December 7, she and David had flown to Fort Ord, near Monterey, California, to entertain the soldiers with Edgar Bergen and Charlie McCarthy on *The Chase and Sanborn Hour*. It was midday when they first heard reports that the Japanese had attacked Pearl Harbor and that the United States was on its way to war.

No changes were made in the *Chase and Sanborn* script. Judy sang, "Zing! Went the Strings of My Heart" and traded quips with Charlie McCarthy, but the proceedings were constantly interrupted by news bulletins. The Roses flew home the next day amid rumors that the Japanese might strike the California mainland next.

On December 23, Judy and David entertained listeners on *The Treasury Hour*, a radio series designed to plug the Allied cause. Judy and Mickey had, in fact, guest-starred on the very first *Treasury* program the previous summer. It was the Fourth of July, and playful Mickey could not resist shooting

off a live firecracker in the studio while Judy read her lines. Now, no one was making jokes.

On New Year's, *Babes on Broadway* opened to enthusiastic reviews. Howard Barnes of the *New York Herald Tribune* called it "brash and engaging entertainment for any holiday season," and critics and fans loved the film's lavish production numbers.

One of Judy's New Year resolutions was to help in the war effort wherever possible, and in January she and David started a three-week tour of various army training camps. In Florida, the couple managed to sandwich in a brief, belated honeymoon, and then it was off to more camps. Finally, at Camp Walters in Mineral Wells, Texas, Judy's voice gave out. Suffering from "strep throat," she was forced to cancel the remainder of the tour.

Although a runaway success like *Babes on Broadway* would have been enough to keep some Hollywood producers resting on their laurels for months,

A crowd of twenty-five thousand gather in Los Angeles's Pershing Square where Judy entertains with patriotic tunes.

Judy and Gene Kelly salute the Two-a-Day (a vaudeville term for two shows a day) in *For Me and My Gal*.

were also a contributing factor. She recalled a day she collapsed at the studio after rehearsing a particularly strenuous dance number:

> The director called the studio doctor and told him I *had* to get through that number that day, as the set was to be dismantled. "Don't worry," said the doctor, "here's something that will pull you through." He produced a bottle of pills and I took some. He told me to go and lie down in my dressing room for ten minutes and I'd feel on top of the world. Sure enough, he was right. But I didn't sleep all that night and arrived at the studio feeling like a wreck. Once again the doc gave me some of the blue pills, but he also gave me a bottle of yellow pills. "If you have any trouble sleeping," he said, "take a couple of these." From that age I've been on sort of a treadmill.

Judy's radio work slackened that spring, and her appearance on *The Chase and Sanborn Hour* on June 21 was her only major network performance. She visited Decca Records in April to record four new numbers, and she returned in July—with Gene Kelly—to do two more.

But not everything in Judy's life was work. On

Arthur Freed had at least three new projects in development—all for Judy. *The Big Time*, a panoramic view of vaudeville, was perhaps the most promising. Set against the backdrop of World War I, *The Big Time*—soon retitled *For Me and My Gal*—portrayed a young female singer who teams up with a rather shady song-and-dance man (Gene Kelly) whose one dream is "to play the big time," the Palace Theatre in New York. The two eventually fall in love and are promised a booking at the Palace, but the war interferes and the man is drafted.

Production started on *For Me and My Gal* on April 3, again with Busby Berkeley directing. Appearing with Judy and Gene were George Murphy, Marta Eggerth, Ben Blue, Richard Quine, and Keenan Wynn.

Judy was looking thin and drawn, which many of her friends and associates attributed to her recent illness. She later told Michael Wilding that drugs

The Gumm Sisters, now the Garland girls, are reunited on the set of Judy's *Presenting Lily Mars* in 1942.

Judy entertains thousands of troops preparing to ship out to the war.

June 10, she celebrated her twentieth birthday, and David gave her sables. The next afternoon they drove up to Lancaster to attend the wedding of a childhood chum. Judy volunteered to sing, "Oh, Promise Me," and David accompanied her on piano.

Judy had a few months off after completing *For Me and My Gal* in May, but MGM made up for it by scheduling two new films to shoot back-to-back beginning in October. Up first was *Presenting Lily Mars*, produced by Joe Pasternak, who had just moved over to Metro from Universal to head a second musicals unit.

Based on a novel by Booth Tarkington, *Lily Mars* was a comedy about a small-town stagestruck girl who eventually makes it big and falls in love with a Broadway producer. The picture had originally been planned as a dramatic vehicle for Lana Turner, but Pasternak and scriptwriters Richard Connell and Gladys Lehman refashioned it as a musical for Judy. Van Heflin costarred as the Broadway producer. Fay Bainter, Richard Carlson, Spring Byington, Marta Eggerth, and Connie Gilcrist were also cast.

On October 12, Judy joined Adolphe Menjou and John Payne in a *Lux Radio Theatre* adaptation of *Morning Glory*, a 1933 Katharine Hepburn film. Judy enjoyed it, and jumped at the chance to return to the series two months later to star as Esther Blodgett in a radio version of *A Star Is Born*.

"Radio's for me!" Judy exclaimed to the press. "I am given chances on the air that I am never given on the screen. I played opposite Walter Pidgeon in 'A Star Is Born,' and there was 'Morning Glory' opposite Adolphe Menjou. People actually called up at home asking, 'Is that really Judy?' "

On Christmas Eve, she appeared on *Command Performance*, a program produced by the War Department for broadcast by shortwave to the troops fighting overseas. The series, started the previous spring, had no budget; it paid no money to anyone— all talent was donated. Stars considered *Command Performance* their contribution to the war effort, and the broadcasts were always booked solid. The Christmas Eve show, a special treat for the home front as well as the troops, was heard in the United States over each of the four major networks.

The next day, Judy appeared with Bob Hope in a ten-minute segment of yet another wartime broadcast, Elgin Watch Company's *Christmas Day Canteen*. A two-hour salute to the U.S. fighting forces, the program also starred Bette Davis, Gracie Fields, Abbott and Costello, Cass Daley, and Don Ameche, who doubled as master of ceremonies. Judy had special reason to feel patriotic that Christmas—David had enlisted in the Army Air Corps.

With the coming of the New Year, Judy started rehearsals for Arthur Freed's new production of *Girl*

Crazy. The picture teamed her again with Mickey Rooney, with Gil Stratton, Robert E. Strickland, June Allyson, Rags Ragland, Nancy Walker, Guy Kibbee, Frances Rafferty, and Tommy Dorsey and his orchestra. Fred Finklehoffe had fashioned a new script that retained the basic plot of the Broadway show (a spoiled New York playboy is sent by his father to an Arizona dude ranch to learn a little humility and good manners), but he softened it a little to accommodate the casting of Mickey and Judy.

Assigned to direct *Girl Crazy* was Busby Berkeley, who had done four Garland/Rooney musicals in four years. This time, however, Berkeley's highly stylized staging (not to mention his stern taskmaster-like work habits) seemed to rub everyone the wrong way. Production began, as usual, with the staging of the musical numbers, and right away there was conflict between Berkeley and Roger Edens over "I Got Rhythm." Edens later explained, "We disagreed basically about the number's presentation. I wanted it rhythmic and simply staged; but Berkeley got his big ensembles and trick cameras into it again, plus a lot of girls in Western outfits, with fringe skirts and people cracking whips, firing guns . . . and cannons going off all over my arrangement and Judy's voice.

Judy and Jack Benny prepare to entertain the boys overseas at a radio show *Command Performance* in 1945.

Judy stars in MGM's remake of George Gershwin's *Girl Crazy.*

Well, we shouted at each other, and I said, 'There isn't enough room on the lot for both of us.' "

Edens won the confrontation—Freed dismissed Berkeley, who moved over to 20th Century-Fox for *The Gang's All Here. Girl Crazy*, minus its director, was shut down for a month while Freed looked for a replacement.

Problems, meanwhile, had developed on *Presenting Lily Mars.* Studio executives and preview audiences had found the film rather dull and were not certain that the woman in the film (Judy/Lily) had actually become a star by the end of the story. Louis B. Mayer thought that the film needed a stronger conclusion.

Charles Walters, a young Broadway dancer who had joined Metro the previous summer to work with Gene Kelly as a dance director on *DuBarry Was a Lady*, was asked to create a new production number—something that could be tacked onto *Lily Mars* to present her as the new toast of Broadway. Walters recalled:

Judy, Mickey, and Tommy Dorsey prepare for Busby Berkeley's elaborate finale to *Girl Crazy* in 1943.

BELOW: Advertising tie-ins authorized by the studio always included a mention of the star's current film.

The studio felt (the picture) needed a more impressive finale—something more sophisticated for Judy to become involved in. . . . So they called me in to stage a new finale, as well as dance with her in it. It was a "Broadway Rhythm" number, with Tommy Dorsey and his band. Irene did Judy's costumes, and they allowed Judy to wear her hair up for the first time. It was all very chic. L. B. Mayer saw it and said to Arthur Freed, the producer, "I wonder if we should put Chuck under contract as a dancer?" and Arthur replied, "No, I think he has more value as a dance director!"

Chuck proved his worth to MGM on this quickie *Lily Mars* assignment. He and Judy worked so well together that "Broadway Rhythm" was finished within a couple of days, and Walters, along with director Norman Taurog, was quickly assigned to Judy's also ailing *Girl Crazy* project.

On February 2, Judy and David confirmed what friends had been speculating about for weeks: they were separating. She still loved him very much, but she loved him more like a brother than a husband. Her biggest worry, she confided to friends, was how to get a divorce without hurting him. "It's best for

both of us to separate," she told the press, "and work out our mutual differences."

The marital status of the whole Garland clan seemed in a state of flux. Mary Jane (Susie) had remarried to Jack Cathcart, the drummer the Gumms had met in Chicago in 1934, and now lived in Las Vegas. Virginia's (Jimmie's) marriage to Bobby Sherwood was about to end in divorce, and even Ethel's marriage to Will Gilmore was on the rocks.

Judy's home on Stone Canyon Drive in Bel Air was sold, and Ethel bought a house on Ogden Drive in Westwood, where she lived with Virginia, Virginia's daughter Judalein, and Ethel's own mother, Judy's Grandma Eva.

With David in the service and a divorce pending, Judy no longer felt comfortable in the huge Harlow mansion. She took a tiny apartment, but, as she later said, "I didn't like to stay alone at night, and there was no room for a maid." When Mary Martin went east to do *One Touch of Venus* on Broadway, Judy leased Mary's house, just a few blocks away from Ethel's new home in Westwood.

Virginia had taken a job at MGM as a script girl. The sisters would have lunch together at the commissary, and, in the evenings when time allowed, Judy babysat Judalein.

Production on *Girl Crazy* stretched into May. In the meantime, Judy, Gene Kelly, and George Murphy recreated *For Me and My Gal* for radio's *Screen Guild Players*. *Command Performance* also beckoned. The War Department series booked Judy, Bing Crosby, and Jimmy Durante for a program, and they performed their signature tunes: Judy sang "Over the Rainbow," Bing sang "The Blue of the Night," and Jimmy sang "Inka Dinka Doo."

Judy, Cary Grant, and Ruth Hussey teamed up for a second *Command Performance*, and Judy and Bing later did an all-music segment of the series. Included were medleys of favorite songs and a duet of "People Will Say We're in Love," from the new Broadway hit, *Oklahoma!*

Presenting Lily Mars opened in theatres around the country in May 1943, just as production was being completed on *Girl Crazy*. Critics loved Judy, as always, but this time they found the film lacking. Even Chuck Walters' big production number did not help.

Judy sings at her first "grown-up" concert at Robin Hood Dell in Philadelphia in 1943.

"Miss Garland is fresh and pretty," wrote the *New York Times*. "She has a perky friendliness that is completely disarming. She is a gifted young lady . . . [But] for all its sweetness, *Presenting Lily Mars* is uninviting fare. . . . Perhaps M-G-M should let Miss Garland grow up and stay that way."

Growing up was foremost in Judy's mind. On June 10, she celebrated her twenty-first birthday, and a party was planned in her honor. She later discussed the proceedings:

My sister, Jimmie, Danny Kaye, Keenan Wynn, Dore Schary, and Betty Asher surprised me by making records of a script they'd written called "The Life of Judy Garland." It began with my first cry, which Danny Kaye gave to the tune of "Over the Rainbow," and continued in a kidding vein to tell me what had happened to me in twenty-one years. It was terribly funny, but it ended with a serious little speech given by Keenan so beautiful that I cried—I was so touched and so happy.

Producer Joe Pasternak, meanwhile, had started work on a new film, *Thousands Cheer*. Originally planned as a small, romantic musical about a soldier (Gene Kelly) and a colonel's daughter (Kathryn Grayson), it emerged as an all-star spectacle. Inter-

41

polated into the story line was an army camp show that featured nearly every face (including Judy's) on the MGM lot. Judy performed a specialty number, created by Roger Edens, that was called "The Joint Is Really Jumpin' Down at Carnegie Hall." She was accompanied by Jose Iturbi, who was making his film debut.

On Thursday evening, July 1, Judy performed in live concert at Robin Hood Dell, an outdoor, bowl-type theatre in Philadelphia. She was the first such Hollywood singer ever to appear there, and she drew the biggest crowd the management had ever seen. Over 25,000 fans showed up, and 10,000 of them had to be turned away. Those lucky enough to stay heard Judy sing everything from her favorite Gershwin songs to "The Joint Is Really Jumpin' . . ." She was backed by the ninety-piece Philadelphia Orchestra under the baton of Andre Kostelanetz.

Judy and Ethel had actually traveled east for a two-week United Service Organization (USO) camp show tour through Pennsylvania and New York. While in Manhattan on July 4, Judy guest-starred,

Judy with her friend James Cagney.

again with Kostelanetz, on his radio show, *The Pause That Refreshes On the Air* (sponsored by Coca-Cola).

Judy's tour for the USO got under way July 8. The USO was thrilled that Judy had agreed to the appearances. "She has such a bright, clean image," a spokesman explained. "The soldiers adore her. The fact that she isn't necessarily a sexpot makes her even more desired. Judy is the girl soldiers want to marry."

Judy returned to California in early August, only to receive yet another invitation for special wartime service. The Hollywood Victory Committee asked Judy to join its Third War Drive, then tooling up for a sixteen-city cross-country swing. Also asked to volunteer were Mickey Rooney, Greer Garson, Dick Powell, James Cagney, Fred Astaire, Lucille Ball, Betty Hutton, Kathryn Grayson, Jose Iturbi, Harpo Marx, Ish Kabibble, Kay Kyser (who served as master of ceremonies), and starlets Doris Merrick, Dorothy Merritt, Rosemary La Planche, and Margie Stewart.

Crowds flooded into Los Angeles' Union Station in mid-September to see the troupe off. Twenty-three days and 10,000 miles later, the Hollywood Cavalcade chugged back into town having sold $1,079,586,819 worth of war bonds. The tour, which formally opened with a broadcast from the White House, played to nearly seven million fans, each of whom had to purchase a $25 bond to gain admittance to a performance. During one memorable noon hour, Judy sang for 8000 employees at the Philadelphia Navy Yard. She urged them to increase their war bond purchases, and they joined her in singing the choruses of her songs.

Thousands Cheer opened in New York on September 13, with the proceeds from the first night's special benefit performance going to the Third War Loan Drive. The box office took in $534,000 that evening, and MGM reaped equally bankable notices in the next day's papers: "It's been a long time since Metro spread itself so lavishly," remarked the *New York Times*. "Musically there is something for all tastes."

Girl Crazy, Judy's big film that autumn, opened in theatres over Thanksgiving weekend. Earlier in the month she had recorded the entire score for

The Third War Loan Bond Tour prepares to leave Los Angeles in 1943. Left to right: Judy, Fred Astaire, Greer Garson, Betty Hutton, Mickey Rooney, Kay Kyser, Lucille Ball, and Harpo Marx.

BELOW: Judy and WAVEs Wilma Leeman, Mary Jane Smith, Edythe Dilg, and Marian Holland watch an aerial demonstration at the U.S. Naval Air Station in Lakehurst, New Jersey, in 1943.

Decca, and the new album ensured that all her fans would soon be humming the tunes of "I Got Rhythm" and "But Not for Me."

"Hold your hats, folks! Mickey Rooney and Judy Garland are back in town!" So began the *New York Times* review of *Girl Crazy*. "Miss Garland's songs, such as 'Bidin' My Time,' should soothe even the most savage beast; of all the child prodigies of Hollywood, Miss Garland has outgrown her adolescence most gracefully and still sings a song with an appealing sincerity which is downright irresistible."

Meet Me in St. Louis, with Vincente Minnelli in line to direct, was scheduled to start production on December 7, 1943. Judy did not want to do the picture. Minnelli recalls, "She thought it would be a mistake to play a seventeen-year-old. She'd just starred in *Presenting Lily Mars*, a picture about a stagestruck girl, and felt it was the first step in her transition from child to adult. To revert back to a teenaged girl in her next film would be a mistake."

For once MGM brass sided with Judy and added the complaint that the shooting script lacked any real plot. Freed knew that the film's story line was

Judy, as Esther Smith, laments the myopia of the boy next door.

fragile—it revolved around an imminent transfer of a father to New York and the effect of the prospective move on the rest of the family. But Freed was adamant—"What I want to make is a simple story, a story that basically says, 'There's no place like home,'" he explained. "I'll make a plot with song and dance and music. That's the way my characters will come to life. I want to make this the most delightful piece of Americana ever. Sets, costumes . . . it'll cost a bit, but it'll be great."

Finally, MGM—and Judy—agreed. After all, they reasoned, the man had been right before.

Ralph Blane and Hugh Martin were hired, and within weeks they composed three songs that would become standards: "The Boy Next Door," "Have Yourself a Merry Little Christmas," and—another permanent addition to Judy's repertoire—"The Trolley Song."

Judy starred in the film as seventeen-year-old Esther Smith. Leon Ames played her father; Mary Astor, her mother; Lucille Bremer, her older sister; Margaret O'Brien and Joan Carroll, her younger sis-

ters; Harry Davenport, her grandfather; Marjorie Main, the family cook; and Tom Drake, the boy next door.

On December 12, Judy made another of her periodic forays into radio drama, costarring with Alan Ladd in "Ringside Table" on CBS's *Silver Theatre.* Judy portrayed a New York nightclub singer; Ladd, an FBI agent posing as a playboy while "shadowing" a suspected enemy agent—the manager of Judy's club.

Christmas Day was Elgin Watch time again, and Judy joined Jack Benny, Bob Hope, Bing Crosby, Lena Horne, Carmen Miranda, and a host of others on a two-hour salute to those in the service overseas and workers on the home front.

Judy's holiday week also included a visit to Decca, where she recorded "No Love, No Nothin'," a popular wartime song, and "Journey to a Star."

During the early months of January, Judy and Vincente Minnelli started to date, and, by April, when he was editing *Meet Me in St. Louis,* they were inseparable. Both wanted to get married; they planned to do so as soon as Judy could obtain a divorce from David Rose. She told the press, "You know it is not possible to divorce a man in service without his permission. I have repeatedly asked Dave to please sign the papers. He is always charming and says he

Judy, Frank Sinatra, and Bing Crosby sing for the troops overseas on the radio show *Command Performance.*

Judy entertains with Edgar Bergen and Effie Klinker on *The Charlie McCarthy Show.*

will, and then he promptly forgets all about it. He was my first love . . . but now I realize we were better apart."

With filming on *Meet Me in St. Louis* complete, Arthur Freed gave his unit a bonus—an all-expenses-paid trip to New York. Judy loved seeing Manhattan through Vincente's sophisticated eyes and was charmed—and challenged—by many of his witty theatrical friends. The vacation was all too brief, and Judy returned to Los Angeles to face perhaps the busiest fifteen months of her career.

First on the docket was a three-day recording session for Decca, where "Meet Me in St. Louis" and five other delightful songs from the film were being packaged as a three-disc set. "The Trolley Song" had "hit" written all over it, and both Bing Crosby and Kate Smith expressed interest in singing it on their respective radio shows.

During the spring and summer of 1944, Judy was very busy with radio appearances. She joined Bing Crosby on two separate broadcasts of *Command Performance*, and the two singers teamed with Jimmy Durante for a segment of another wartime overseas series, *Mail Call*, for which the threesome did a novelty number entitled, "The Groaner, The Canary, and The Nose." Crosby later reflected on these years: "Judy Garland. She was a great, great comedienne,

and she could do more things than any girl I ever knew—act, sing, dance, and make you laugh. She was everything."

Judy appeared on Frank Sinatra's radio program May 24; a *Salute to the Armed Forces*, June 4; *Everything for the Boys*, July 11; *Your All Time Hit Parade*, August 13; and *The Chase and Sanborn Hour*, June 25 and September 3.

In mid-June, Judy was awarded her interlocutory divorce decree from David Rose. She testified in Superior Court that conflicts between their two careers had made a happy marriage impossible. "We were happy for the first few months," she said, "and then our careers began to conflict. His work kept him away from home a great deal." By California law, it would take the divorce twelve months to become final.

Arthur Freed had been toying for two years with the idea of creating a film version of the Ziegfeld Follies. Now, in 1944, Louis B. Mayer gave the project his blessing. The year was to mark MGM's twentieth anniversary, and Mayer felt such a picture would make an ideal vehicle in which to showcase the studio's abundant talent. The picture would have no ongoing plot but, like a vaudeville show, would be divided into some twenty sketches and musical numbers, just like the real Ziegfeld shows, each spotlighting one or more big-name MGM stars.

Production had gotten under way in March while Judy and Vincente were finishing *St. Louis.* In early July, with that film finally complete, Freed asked both to make *Ziegfeld Follies of 1944.*

Various bits of material were discussed for Judy, only one of which actually wound up on film—a sketch that had actually been prepared for and rejected by someone else. "Madame Crematon," or, as it is also known, "A Great Lady Has an Interview," a rather sophisticated sketch written by Roger Edens and Kay Thompson, was conceived with Greer Garson in mind for the title role, but her husband thought it beneath her. Judy stepped in, and Chuck Walters staged it for her. The routine took ten days to rehearse, one day to record, and three days to film—between July 7 and 22. Nine days later, Judy was back at Metro ready to start work on yet another Freed picture, *The Clock.*

Based on a simple love story Freed had discovered some eighteen months earlier, *The Clock* teamed Judy with Robert Walker, and was her first non-musical film assignment. For months Judy had been coaxing MGM to let her try her hand at a straight dramatic part. The plot concerned a young New Yorker who meets a soldier in Pennsylvania Station; they fall in love, get married, and say goodbye (he's off to war)—all within the span of two days.

Production started August 1, with Fred Zinneman directing. Judy secretly wanted Minnelli to guide her through her paces, and for the next three weeks, while Vincente finished his *Follies* assignments, she made life uncomfortable on the *Clock* set. It was not difficult to see what she was up to, so Freed formally offered the picture to Minnelli. He accepted and started everything over on September 1.

Appearing with Judy and Walker were Keenan Wynn, James and Lucille Gleason, Marshall Thompson, and Ruth Brady, and the city of New York. "My plan," explained Minnelli, "was to develop New York as a third major character."

Roger Edens did a cameo as a pianist in a restaurant scene, and Choo-Choo, Judy's pet poodle, did a walk-on—in his case, a run-on—in one of the crowd scenes in the railway station.

By this time Judy was living at home again with Ethel. "It isn't much fun coming home after a long working day to an empty house," she explained later. "I had moved into Mary Martin's house in Westwood. She was in New York for *One Touch of Venus*, and she decided to sell the house. A doctor acquaintance went into the Navy, so I leased his house for six months." A bout with the flu forced Judy to move into Ethel's house in Westwood, and she enjoyed having her family around so much that she decided to stay. Susie and Jack Cathcart, too, moved in for a while, and the three Gumm Sisters were again under one roof.

Production of *The Clock* wrapped November 21, just as *Meet Me in St. Louis* was opening to Thanksgiving audiences. The *New York Daily News* gave *St. Louis* four stars and recommended it to anyone "looking for a picture that represents sheer, unadulterated enjoyment," and Bosley Crowther of the *New York Times* remarked that Judy's voice "grows

Judy prepares for her "Interview" sequence in *Ziegfeld Follies of 1946* (actually filmed in 1944).

riper and more expressive in each new film. Her chortling of 'The Trolley Song' puts fresh zip into that inescapable tune," and, drawing on an expression used in the movie, called it "a ginger peachy show." Audiences everywhere agreed.

The week of December 11, Judy appeared on the cover of *Life* magazine. In another publication, she explained her ongoing relationship with Vincente Minnelli. She told columnist Adela Rogers St. Johns:

I made one mistake, I don't want to make another. I love my work. I know there are girls who can give up their work and get married and just live at home. I don't believe I could. I don't believe I'd be happy. So I have to have someone that understands about me and my work and thinks it's important and—we have to work together. Vincente is wonderful. He's the most interesting man I've ever known. I don't know yet—maybe it will be right for us. We both know that a marriage can either be the most wonderful thing on earth or it can gum up your whole life and spoil everything. We're thinking it over.

The year 1945 brought no respite from the busy schedule: January's calendar alone included a recording session at Decca, an appearance on a radio special saluting Franklin Roosevelt's birthday, and rehearsals for an expensive new film, *The Harvey Girls*.

On February 15, Judy joined an all-star cast to record for *Command Performance* a gala production of "Dick Tracy." The formal title of the show was "Dick Tracy in B-flat, *or* For Goodness' Sake, Isn't He Ever Going to Marry Tess Trueheart?" Judy was cast as a character named Snowflake; Bing Crosby played Tracy; Bob Hope appeared as Flat Top; Frank Sinatra, as Shaky; Jimmy Durante, as Mole; Dinah Shore, as Tess Trueheart; Jerry Colonna, as the chief of police.

MGM had postponed release of *Ziegfeld Follies* indefinitely. A preview held in November had proven disastrous. L. B. Mayer ordered the film revised,

Judy, costumed for her role in *The Clock*, appears on her first cover of *Life*.

Judy vacations in Carmel during production of *The Clock* in 1944.

and another preview was scheduled for midspring.

Planning ahead, Arthur Freed had two additional projects in development that winter. One, *The Belle of New York*, he had earmarked for Judy and Fred Astaire. "I'm thrilled beyond words," Judy told the press. "Imagine dancing with Fred Astaire!"

Astaire, however, felt the *Belle* script weak and opted for Freed's other project, *Yolanda and the Thief*, instead. A fairy tale about a young heiress who becomes attracted to a roguish adventurer, *Yolanda* was also of interest to Vincente Minnelli. With both Vincente and Fred excited about it, Judy wanted to be in *Yolanda*, too. Freed, however, had his own protégé, Lucille Bremer, in mind for the starring role. Also, Judy was already committed to *The Harvey Girls*, and *Yolanda* had been scheduled to start production before *Harvey Girls* wrapped. Finally Judy agreed that *Harvey* provided perhaps the better part, and production got under way. *Yolanda and the Thief* turned out to be such a disappointment that Fred Astaire decided to make just one more film—*Blue Skies* for Paramount—and then retire.

Judy with her second husband Vincente Minnelli on their wedding day.

The script for *The Harvey Girls* concerned the young women who served as waitresses in the Fred Harvey restaurant chain, which stretched from Topeka, Kansas, through the Old Southwest, in the 1880s. These young women were considered to have good character, as opposed to the "loose ladies" who worked in most saloons and public houses.

Judy, Cyd Charisse, and Virginia O'Brien starred as "the good girls," Angela Lansbury as the wanton competition, and John Hodiak as the love interest caught in the middle. Also in the cast were Ray Bolger, Preston Foster, Kenny Baker, Marjorie Main, and Chill Wills.

George Sidney directed *The Harvey Girls,* and Roger Edens was associate producer. Harry Warren and Johnny Mercer wrote the music, including a production number destined to be Judy's next big hit— "On the Atcheson, Topeka, and the Santa Fe."

Production on *The Harvey Girls* lasted nearly five months, taking its toll on Judy, who had been working nonstop for nearly a year. Production records indicate that she often reported to work late and, occasionally, not at all. Biographer Christopher Finch, in *Rainbow,* later recalled that her pattern of lateness became so taken for granted that on the few occa-

sions she did show up on time, everyone was flabbergasted. Judy explained how her busy work schedule—and studio politics—had taken their toll: "I was a nervous wreck, jumpy and irritable from sleeping too little. I couldn't take the tension at the studio. Everything at MGM was competition. Every day I went to work with tears in my eyes. Work gave me no pleasure. The studio had become a haunted house for me. It was all I could do to keep from screaming every time the director looked at me."

On May 14, Judy borrowed time from her film schedule to record a couple of sides for Decca. MGM was furious when the Decca sessions ran late into the night, causing Judy to miss sleep and have to cancel the next day's shooting. Too many obligations were clearly pulling at Judy. There never seemed to be enough time.

The Harvey Girls completed production on June 4. Vincente had finished *Yolanda* a couple of weeks earlier. Now, with some breathing room, the two began to plan their wedding. Judy's divorce from David Rose became final on June 8, and she and Vincente considered dashing off to New York to wed. Louis B. Mayer, however, had his heart set on giving the bride away, and, because he could not make the trip east, the wedding was rescheduled to take place in Ethel's backyard.

For her wedding dress, Judy chose a gray silk jersey, cut along Renaissance lines, and wore a small Renaissance bonnet of fine veiling. She carried a bouquet of pink and white peonies. Reverend William E. Roberts of the Beverly Hills Community Presbyterian Church presided—then had to dash back to his church to marry MGM starlet Donna Reed and her fiancé, Tony Owen. A couple of hours later, both couples, the Minnellis and the Owens, departed for New York on the same train, the Santa Fe Super Chief.

The Clock opened in theatres May 25 and was welcomed by the *New York Times* as "a tender and refreshingly simple drama . . . the kind of picture that leaves one with a warm feeling toward his fellow man." The *New York Herald Tribune* applauded Judy for her first nonsinging role, and the *Daily News* called the film "the sweetest, most tender comedy drama yet produced about a soldier and a girl." Judy later commented, "It just missed being great. The critics said it proved I could hold up my end without a forty-piece band, and that was gratifying."

The Minnellis' extended honeymoon in New York was delightful. "It was the first time in more years than I could remember that I just relaxed and had fun and let somebody else take care of me," Judy confessed later.

The Minnellis spent much of their time in New York seeing shows and catching up with old friends. One evening he mentioned his fondness for *The Pirate*, in which Lunt and Fontanne had starred on Broadway a few seasons earlier. He decided to ask Freed about doing a musical version of the piece.

Judy—being Judy—could not avoid work. She attended a recording session for Decca, and, on August 10, appeared on CBS's *Jerry Wayne Show*. "A Garland of Songs for You," promised the ads, with Judy and Jerry harmonizing with the Jeff Alexander Orchestra.

Judy still loved radio, and she was delighted to learn that at least one of the major networks wanted her for a regular weekly series. Such assignments were still verboten according to her MGM contract, but the prospect of radio—and stage—work was intriguing. "I am not going to re-sign with the studio when my contract expires," she announced one day. "Oh, they've been wonderful to me at MGM, but I want to go on the stage. I was in vaudeville so many years when I was Frances Gumm, and I miss the sound of applause. If I could get a play on the order of *Lady in the Dark*, a drama or a comedy with music, I would be terribly happy."

The Minnellis returned to Los Angeles after a brief excursion to Boston, where one of Vincente's films was opening, and Judy, rather quickly, went back to work. On September 7 and 10, she recorded four more of the *Harvey Girls* tunes for Decca and, on October 5, appeared with Frank Sinatra as substitute cohosts of *The Danny Kaye Show*—Kaye was away on a USO tour.

Judy was also scheduled to start work that month on a new Arthur Freed all-star spectacular, *Till the Clouds Roll By*, with Robert Walker, who would be starring as composer Jerome Kern. But Judy and Vincente had news for Freed: Judy was pregnant.

A makeshift production schedule was prepared, and Judy was allowed to film all her scenes first,

within a span of two weeks. Although Richard Whorf had been assigned to direct the picture, Vincente again handled Judy's scenes himself. She had been cast as Broadway star Marilyn Miller, and was given three Kern numbers: "Sunny," "Look for the Silver Lining," and "Who?" (A fourth number, "D'Ya Love Me?" was recorded and filmed but later deleted.)

Production went well. In late October Judy started what would be a year-long hiatus from MGM—her longest vacation since her contract was signed ten years earlier. Why had she allowed herself such grueling schedules? "Acting was the only place where I felt like a useful person, where people said, 'Fine, you did a good job. Come again,' and everybody needs to hear those things."

She still had some radio work to do—Jerome Kern died suddenly, and, on December 9, she and other *Clouds* alumni appeared on a memorial broadcast. In January, she starred in an adaptation of *The Clock* on *Lux Radio Theatre*. But for once, Judy had something other than a job to fulfill her needs.

Judy asks the musical question "Who?" in Arthur Freed's biography of Jerome Kern, *Till the Clouds Roll By*.

OVERLEAF: Portrait by John Engstead.

5

Judy had a little-girl quality—a vulnerability that made audiences want to reach out to her, embrace her, and protect her from the wicked world outside.

RADIE HARRIS

Judy's year away from the cameras gave her deserved rest and the opportunity to play homebody. The first few weeks were spent remodeling the Minnelli house. Vincente lived on a hill high above Beverly Hills on Evanview Drive. It was spacious for one, cozy for two, and totally inadequate for a family. Judy decided to redecorate. She and Vincente rented a house in Malibu Beach and had the Evanview home totally redone.

On March 12, 1946, Judy gave birth by cesarean section to Liza May Minnelli. Vincente deluged the hospital with flowers, and each day thereafter sent Judy a tiny white bouquet. Liza was the greatest thing that ever happened to either of them. "We were wild over Liza from the first moment we laid eyes on her," said Judy proudly.

Two MGM releases kept Judy's name in the papers that spring: *The Harvey Girls*, which opened January 18, and the now-retitled *Ziegfeld Follies of 1946*, which premiered March 15.

Reviewing *Harvey Girls*, Howard Barnes of the *New York Herald Tribune* called Judy "the film's bright star" who is "effectively glamorized in get-ups of the '90's and sings her songs pleasantly." *Ziegfeld Follies* turned out to be something of a white elephant, but many critics loved Judy's "Madame Crematon" number. *Newsweek* noted her "unexpected flair for occupational satire."

Not everyone concurred: Joe Pihonda of the *Herald Tribune* warned, "The fashion of the big-screen revue has seen its day. The person who gets the worst flogging in the deal is Judy Garland. Wound up in a sketch called The Interview, Miss Garland has some mighty unpleasant stuff to do." For years, Judy fans would debate the issue.

On July 17, Judy guest-starred on Bob Crosby's radio show, and three days later appeared live on stage at a "Jerome Kern Memorial Concert" held in the Hollywood Bowl.

At the studio, work was progressing on *The Pirate*, which everyone agreed would be Judy's back-to-work picture. Gene Kelly had been set to costar, and Cole Porter had agreed to write the music. Albert Hackett and Frances Goodrich were busy adapting S. N. Behrman's play for the screen.

In September, Judy helped *Hollywood Startime* inaugurate a new radio series of motion-picture adaptations on CBS. She starred as Linda in a new production of *Holiday*, a 1938 film made famous by Katharine Hepburn.

Judy prepares to rehearse *Drive In* radio drama for director William Spier and his wife, Kay Thompson, in 1946.

ABC heralds their weekly *Bing Crosby Philco Radio Time* in various papers around the country in 1946.

Judy recorded a total of five new tunes for Decca that autumn, then returned to CBS for something she had long desired—a starring role on writer-producer Bill Spier's hit dramatic series, *Suspense*. "I'd wanted to appear on *Suspense* for some time," Judy announced, "but just the right script didn't come up. When it did, I was anxious to get at it immediately. I would have learned it word for word a week in advance to prove to Bill I wouldn't let him down, but he gave me the same treatment they all get on that wonderful show. My script arrived the day before the rehearsal to make sure I'd do it the way the producer wanted it—not the way Garland thought it should be."

Spier, incidentally, was then married to Judy's vocal coach Kay Thompson. "She's my best critic and severest friend," Judy said. The Spiers and the Minnellis were a happy foursome.

At MGM, executives anxiously awaited Judy's return. On November 21, the studio discarded Judy's existing contract and offered her a new seven-year deal, raising her current salary from $3000 to over $5000 per week. The deal, generous as it seemed, would prove to be a mixed blessing—it provided security and a testament of good faith, but it also required seven more years of early-morning makeup calls, scripts to memorize, wardrobe tests, and shooting schedules.

The studio knew that Judy's taste had changed over the years—as had that of many postwar moviegoers. Simple little "backyard musicals" were def-

Judy and Margaret O'Brien re-create "Meet Me in St. Louis" on *Lux Radio Theatre* in 1946.

initely a thing of the past. MGM had some big plans lined up for Judy, including a possible musical remake of *Cimarron* that would costar Gene Kelly. Up first, however, would be Garland and Kelly in *The Pirate*.

The 1946 holiday season seemed like old home week for Judy. She celebrated Thanksgiving by appearing with Bing Crosby on his new ABC radio series, then, in December, she, Margaret O'Brien, and Tom Drake gathered at CBS for a new *Lux Radio Theatre* production of *Meet Me in St. Louis*.

Till the Clouds Roll By opened January 3 to mixed reviews but box office gold. Critics objected most vehemently to the obviously fictionalized biography of Jerome Kern, but everyone seemed to love the lavish production numbers. "Why did Metro cook up such a phony yarn?" lamented Bosley Crowther in the *New York Times*. "Why couldn't it simply have given us more such enjoyable things as Judy Garland playing Marilyn Miller and singing the melodious 'Sunny' and 'Who'?"

The Pirate was gearing up for production at MGM beginning in late November. It was about a nineteenth-century girl (Manuela) who fantasizes about being in love with Mack the Black Macoco, a notorious pirate. Meanwhile, Serafin, a traveling actor, falls in love with fair Manuela, and when she resists his attentions, he masquerades as the man of her dreams. Judy was cast as Manuela; Gene Kelly, as Serafin; Walter Slezak, as the real Black Macoco; and Gladys Cooper, as Manuela's aunt.

Judy started work on the new picture on December 2, prerecording the songs Cole Porter had written for her and Gene. Minnelli recalls, "Judy was ready to give *The Pirate* her all. The picture would show her comedic range. She was quite certain she'd fly through the filming. It was going to be such a lovely labor that there'd be no need for amphetamines and barbiturates to see her through. . . . She'd show the people at the studio . . . she would deliver."

But Judy did not deliver—at least not without a great many delays. Shooting started on February 17, but, as Gene Kelly later recalled, "Judy had periods when she didn't show up on the set. This was my first indication something was wrong."

Judy had lost her confidence. She would lock herself in her dressing room and tell her dresser, "I just wouldn't be good enough today. I know it in my bones." Words of encouragement, usually from Vincente, would bring her around. "Just dress and make up," he would say, "and come down and see how you feel. If you still think you aren't up to a job today, we'll change the schedule and shoot around you."

Such schedule shuffling was impossible when it came time to shoot Judy's production numbers, and one complicated dance routine with tropical rhythms and meticulous steps nearly brought on a nervous breakdown. "She began to feel she wasn't functioning," Minnelli explained later, "and turned to the pills that had sustained her during past crises." The medicine, in turn, made her performance much too intense. None of the usual Garland subtleties was there which discouraged Judy, who was always very objective about her own work.

For the next few months, Judy spent as much time away from the set as on it, leaving Minnelli in an impossible position. As director, he was furious; as husband, he was concerned. Finally, on August 14,

shooting appeared to be complete. Judy, long overdue for a rest, checked into a sanitarium near Compton, California, then transferred to one in Stockbridge, Massachusetts. She had to get a grip on things.

A few weeks later, Judy telephoned her manager, Carleton Alsop. "I have found such peace!" she beamed. "I can eat and I want to eat! I can sleep and I never think of taking a sleeping pill! I feel like a new woman!"

Unfortunately, that was all MGM needed to hear. A private screening of *The Pirate* had already labeled the film unreleasable. There would have to be changes—more retakes, new scenes added, old ones replaced—as soon as possible. Intensifying matters, yet another Garland film, Irving Berlin's *Easter Parade*, had been scheduled to start production that fall.

Judy returned to California in October, ready to work. *The Pirate* retakes required approximately two months (October 21 through December 19), with preliminary work on *Easter Parade* starting on November 25. For three weeks, Judy, Kelly, and Min-

Judy and Fred Astaire visit with writer Sidney Sheldon, who collaborated on the screenplay of Irving Berlin's *Easter Parade*.

nelli shuttled back and forth between the two projects. Then, in early December, one of Judy's psychiatrists dropped in to see Freed. He suggested that Vincente be taken off the new picture. It was not in Judy's best interests, the doctor felt, for Vincente to be both husband and director. She needed someone at home in whom she could confide, someone to rely on, someone who could not be construed as "the alter ego of MGM." Freed had to agree, and he replaced Minnelli with Judy's pal Chuck Walters.

Walters, in the years since *Ziegfeld Follies*, had completed his first directorial assignment, Freed's long-postponed *Good News*, with June Allyson in the role once discussed for Judy. Chuck later admitted, "I never had any problems with Judy. We were very close—in fact, we almost got married once! She was always very cooperative. Just toss Judy the ball, and she carried it for a home run. She never went 'glamour girl' on you."

More changes were in the wind for *Easter Parade*: Gene Kelly dropped out after breaking his ankle during a game of touch football, and Cyd Charisse, who was supposed to play "the other woman," likewise withdrew when she fell and pulled a tendon in her leg. Freed placed a call to Fred Astaire, who had retired from pictures a couple of years earlier, and Fred jumped at the chance to work with Garland and Berlin. Ann Miller, who had been hoofing her way through countless "B musicals" at RKO and Columbia, was hired to replace Charisse, but she, too, was nursing a bad back. Peter Lawford, Jules Munshin, and Clinton Sundberg, all relatively healthy, completed the cast.

The plot, a delightful show business confection, concerned a dancer (Astaire) who, when deserted by his longtime partner (Miller), bets a friend (Lawford) that he can pick any showgirl at random and turn her into a star. He chooses one (Judy, of course), accomplishes his task (after a rather rocky start), and winds up falling in love with her—all in time for Easter.

The real joy of the film lay in the Irving Berlin production numbers, including what would become one of Astaire and Garland's most famous routines, "A Couple of Swells." "Judy always loved that number," recalled Chuck Walters. "Garland and Astaire

as a couple of deadbeats, for God's sake! All I had to do was stand back and let it happen." In fact, Judy helped design the tramp costumes for the number. When the wardrobe department presented her with their original ideas, she scowled. "This isn't half gruesome enough," she insisted. She found a size forty tuxedo, had it torn up and resewn, found a mangy-looking wig, and suggested a tooth or two be blacked out. She was delighted by the ludicrous effect it all achieved.

Production ended on *Easter Parade* on February 7, and a sneak preview three weeks later provided a clue to the studio that they had a major hit on their hands. Freed immediately started to work on a sequel.

Judy spent much of the spring of 1948 catching up on her chores as wife and mother and her work on the radio. In May she was a guest on NBC's *Chesterfield Supper Club*, and in June she visited the same network's *Tex and Jinx Show*, a husband-and-wife interview program starring Jinx Falkenberg and John McCrary.

For a while there would be no more recording sessions. After ten years and 84 songs, Judy's contract with Decca had run out. Her last two sides for them ("Nothing But You" and the wistful "I Wish I Were in Love Again") had been recorded on November 15, 1947.

As usual, Arthur Freed had a number of projects waiting for Judy at MGM, the most important being a new Betty Comden–Adolph Green script, *The Barkleys of Broadway*, the project Freed had designed to be the modern-day followup to *Easter Parade*. Astaire had agreed to do the film, as had director Chuck Walters. Rehearsals were scheduled to begin on June 14.

Both *The Pirate* and *Easter Parade* were released in close succession that summer, the quality of *Easter* making up for the disappointment of *Pirate*. *The Pirate* failed to excite audiences the way previous Garland musicals had. Critics, however, found the change-of-pace film exciting. *Newsweek* heralded it as "one of the most delightful musicals to hit the screen in a month of Sundays."

Easter Parade, as predicted, won 3½ stars from the *New York Daily News*, and *Seventeen* magazine voted it "The Picture of the Month." Howard Barnes, of the *New York Herald Tribune*, wrote, "Astaire is hoofing more superbly than ever and Miss Garland is giving him the staunchest of support. Miss Garland has matured to a remarkable degree in *Easter Parade* . . . a handsome and knowing actress. Her latest film performance is altogether her best."

Judy reported for work on *The Barkleys of Broadway* as scheduled and was delighted to be reunited with her *Easter Parade* cohorts. "Let's do it again" was the company's challenge. In the new film, Fred and Judy would portray modern-day Broadway musical comedy stars who have a major falling-out after he criticizes her desire to try her hand at a dramatic play. They separate, and she starts to work on her new show, unaware that Fred is watching from the sidelines. Of course, they both soon realize how much they need each other, and, in the end, they dance off to live happily ever after.

Music for *The Barkleys* had been written by Harry Warren and Ira Gershwin, and these numbers were what the company started to rehearse first. All went well the first week; the second week proved a bit shakier; the third week was *The Pirate* revisited. Judy was simply not ready to tackle such an important new project. On July 12, MGM replaced her with Ginger Rogers.

Officially suspended from her contract, Judy returned to the studio to do two numbers for *Words and Music:* "Johnny One Note" and "I Wish I Were in Love Again," a duet, her last screen appearance, with old buddy Mickey Rooney. The song was one that had been omitted from Judy and Mickey's earlier film, *Babes in Arms*.

Radio appearances with Bing Crosby and Al Jolson kept Judy active in September and early October, and, on October 11, she returned to MGM to start a new film, *In the Good Old Summertime*. She was starting with a clean slate, working with none of the people who had witnessed her erratic behavior a few months earlier. Joe Pasternak was producing the picture, with Robert Z. Leonard directing. Van Johnson had been set to costar, and S. Z. "Cuddles" Sakall, Spring Byington, Buster Keaton, Clinton Sundberg, and—in an unbilled cameo—Liza Minnelli completed the cast.

A musical remake of the 1940 hit *The Shop Around the Corner, In the Good Old Summertime* was set in a Chicago music shop, circa 1900. It was a tale about a young couple who are antagonistic fellow workers, but who unwittingly carry on a correspondence love affair.

Arguably a less important picture than *Barkleys, Summertime* was devoid of the unspoken pressure to recreate or surpass the success of *Easter Parade*. Filming went so well that the production finished five days ahead of schedule. "What did you do to Judy?" asked Louis B. Mayer jubilantly. "We made her feel needed," explained Van Johnson. "We joked with her and kept her happy."

Waiting on MGM's back burner was a film version of Irving Berlin's Broadway smash, *Annie Get Your Gun*. With *In the Good Old Summertime* completed, the studio booked rehearsals to start on the new picture in early March. Judy was cast as Annie Oakley; Howard Keel, as sharpshooter Frank Butler; and Frank Morgan as the proprietor of a Wild West show, Buffalo Bill.

Annie was a comic love story in buckskins, with a lot of toe-tapping music to help get the two stars together before fade-out. Freed had originally asked Chuck Walters to direct, but Chuck's contract was up for renewal, and when his negotiations with the front office dragged on, Freed brought in the old taskmaster himself, Busby Berkeley, who had not worked with Judy since *Girl Crazy*.

Rehearsals started well, but Judy—all too aware of the money and prestige riding on this picture—was clearly unsure of herself. As Hugh Fordin points out, "This was the first time in her career that she was not doing 'a Judy Garland picture.' " Berkeley, never known for eliciting subtle performances, offered little support. Instead, he instigated a rigorous production schedule for Judy and the entire company to meet. The more apprehensive Judy became, the more she turned to medication to calm her nerves. The vicious cycle again.

Filming started April 3, 1949 and was shut down May 3, not because of Judy, who readily admitted that she was not doing her best, but because of Berkeley, who, Freed later confessed, "had no conception of what the picture was all about. He was

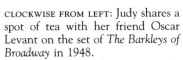

CLOCKWISE FROM LEFT: Judy shares a spot of tea with her friend Oscar Levant on the set of *The Barkleys of Broadway* in 1948.
Judy and gossip columnist Louella Parsons on the set of *In the Good Old Summertime*.
Judy and producer Arthur Freed on the set of *Words and Music*, a biography of Rodgers and Hart.
Judy guest-stars with the great Al Jolson on NBC's *Kraft Music Hall* in 1948.

shooting the whole thing like a stage play. Everyone would come out of the wings, say their lines, and back away upstage for their exits."

Berkeley was out, and MGM again solicited Chuck Walters. Judy's self-confidence, however, could not be so easily mended. "It's too late, Chuck," she cried. "I haven't got the energy . . . or the *nerve* anymore." Walters checked the footage Berkeley had shot and was as dismayed as Judy. "He was such a brute with her . . . it was horrible. Judy had never been worse. She couldn't decide whether she was Mary Martin, Ethel Merman, Martha Raye, or herself. She didn't know who the hell she was."

Chuck tried to start the film over, but Judy was just not up for it. She started to arrive late and leave early, claiming illness. Finally, on May 10, MGM

ABOVE: In an Indian costume for the never-completed *Annie Get Your Gun*, 1949.

Judy, as Annie Oakley, prepares to star in *Annie Get Your Gun*. Betty Hutton got the part.

released her from the picture. Betty Hutton replaced her.

Judy's relationship with her mother was also at a new low. Whenever the two visited, they inevitably wound up fighting. Susie and Jack Cathcart had moved back to Las Vegas, and Jimmie, now married to John Thompson, Jr., had set up housekeeping in Dallas. Unable to help Judy, Ethel decided that she, too, would give Texas a try.

Judy wanted to get away, too. On May 29, she entered Harvard's Peter Bent Brigham Hospital in Boston. Overwrought and exhausted, she wanted nothing more than a good, long rest.

Carleton Alsop quickly reassured Judy's friends that her doctors had found nothing organically wrong. A few weeks later he reported that Judy had started to make day trips into Boston, had visited the seashore, and had even thrown the first ball in an intercity baseball game. "She's begun to burst with good health," Alsop reported, "good health, good spirits, and good humor."

In the Good Old Summertime opened in theatres in June and received excellent notices. One reviewer called it "a rare treat. It's Judy's best picture in years, and her singing is better than first rate—it's sensational, grand entertainment."

Judy returned to Los Angeles in August, anxious to feel productive again. Her fear of not being able to deliver was exceeded only by her fear of having nothing to do. She wanted most of all to please— and to be loved by—her family, her studio, her fans. MGM had *Summer Stock* waiting.

It seemed like a safe picture. She would be surrounded by old friends. Gene Kelly (who originally dismissed the script as "*Babes on Broadway* in a barn") had agreed to costar, and old friends like Marjorie Main, Phil Silvers, Eddie Bracken, and Gloria DeHaven would be around for support. Chuck Walters (who had been replaced in *Annie* by George Sidney) had agreed to direct, and, just to be on the safe side, a psychiatrist friend had been placed on call.

Unfortunately, Judy really was not well enough to be tackling another major film so soon. During her eleven weeks in Boston she had gained weight, and MGM now expressed concern over how she looked on the screen. Once again she turned to diet pills to help her reduce. The pills led to sleeping medication, and before long Judy had missed an important day's work. Walters and Kelly went out of their way to accommodate her (at one point the film was put on a 1 P.M. to 7 P.M. shooting schedule), and she responded with warmth and exuberance. She wanted so much to please.

"The thing about Judy," Gene later explained, "was that she only worked when she thought she was going to be good. If she felt she wasn't up to giving her best, she didn't appear on the set."

The script, as Kelly had warned, was indeed *Babes on Broadway* in a barn. It presented Judy as a New England farmer whose actress-sister invites a New York theatrical troupe to take over the family barn and turn it into a summer theatre. There were, of course, plenty of musical moments to keep the audience interested while Judy and Gene first fight, then fall in love.

Throughout the production of *Summer Stock*, the Hollywood trade papers were chock-full of news about prospective Garland projects. Metro had a lavish production of *Show Boat* planned for her, and Par-

Judy prepares for her last MGM production number in *Summer Stock*.

amount hoped to borrow her services for a Bing Crosby picture. In January, English producer Lew Grade offered her $14,000 per week to play the London Palladium that next summer. But nothing seemed more important to Judy than finishing the picture she had already started.

Summer Stock completed production in early March, and Judy dashed off to Carmel for a vacation and to finish slimming down. Walters and Joe Pasternak, meanwhile, screened the picture's existing footage and decided it was *Lily Mars* all over again: it needed a final production number, something memorable like "A Couple of Swells" from *Easter Parade*. Chuck called Judy long distance, and she knew immediately what she wanted to add. She had recently heard her old friend Harold Arlen sing his "Get Happy" number at a party. Could she sing that?

MGM bought the rights, Judy came home rested and remarkably slim, Walters rehearsed his male dancers, and, when all was ready, Judy came in and shot the whole number in two days. It would be one of her finest moments on film.

Judy was buoyant over "Get Happy" and overjoyed by her new figure. She was so excited that when MGM reneged on their original promise of six months off between pictures, she agreed to do *Royal Wedding*. *Wedding*, an Arthur Freed production starring Fred Astaire, had been planned with June Allyson in mind for the female lead (the role of Fred's sister). Keenan Wynn had been cast as twin brothers; Peter Lawford, as the romantic interest for Allyson; and Sarah Churchill, the romantic interest for Astaire. Tying the whole package together was Chuck Walters, delighted by any opportunity to work with his idol, the great Astaire. Then the unthinkable happened—June became pregnant and had to beg off.

Freed thought immediately of Judy. Walters, however, balked at working with Garland again so soon, and, Astaire or no Astaire, he resigned. Freed replaced him with Stanley Donen.

Judy's first week of rehearsals went well, as did the second. The third week included a twenty-eighth birthday party for her; everything seemed fine. Then, during the fourth week, Judy announced that she could only work half-days for a while. When Donen

scheduled an important rehearsal for Saturday, June 17, she refused to come in at all. MGM had no choice but to suspend her. It soon replaced her on the picture with Jane Powell. Judy, her confidence again shattered, locked herself in a bathroom and put a broken glass to her throat.

"I felt humiliated and unwanted," she confessed later. "And I was faced with the bitter knowledge that I'd come to that unhappy position by my own actions. All my newfound hope evaporated, and all I could see ahead was more confusion. I wanted to black out the future as well as the past. I didn't want to live anymore. I wanted to hurt myself and others.

"Yet even while I stood there in the bathroom with a shattered glass in my hand, and Vincente and my adored secretary, Tully, were pounding on the door, I knew I couldn't solve anything by running away—and that's what killing yourself is. I let them in and tried to make them understand how sorry I was."

Summer Stock, to no one's surprise, opened to good reviews and even better box office. Fans who had been reading about Judy's troubles were anxious to see her again. With time, this would become a pattern: the bigger her setback, the more loyal the fans! The *New York Daily News* reported, "If audience reaction is an indication, *Summer Stock* . . . will give the year's best musical comedies lively competition. Judy and Gene are in fine form." All agreed that "Get Happy" was a knockout.

Judy needed all the encouragement she could get. The reviews lifted her spirits. Ethel flew back from Texas to be at her side. Friends, Katharine Hepburn, for one, visited and urged Judy onto her feet again. "Now listen," Kate reportedly said defiantly, "you're one of the three greatest talents in the world. And your ass has hit the gutter. There's no place to go but up. Now, goddammit, get up and do it!"

Fred Finklehoffe, Judy's friend who had written so many of her screenplays, sent a wire: "Dear Judy, So glad you cut your throat. All the other girl singers needed this kind of break." Judy laughed for days.

Arthur Freed, Judy's champion for over fifteen

years, sent word that she would always have a place in his unit. His new production of *Show Boat* would be ready to start soon, and next year, maybe, they could tackle a screen version of *South Pacific*. Wouldn't that be wonderful?

For once, Judy said no. Vincente was thinking about going to Europe soon to start work with Gene Kelly on *An American in Paris*. Perhaps she and Liza would go, too, for a vacation. The kind of musicals Freed was proposing were supercolossal productions, expensive extravaganzas designed to compete with television. They would bring with them too much pressure . . . too much work. There had been little else than work for so long.

In September, Judy sent her doctor to see Louis B. Mayer and ask that her studio contract be canceled. Legend would have it that MGM fired Garland—perhaps writers felt it made her more of a victim that way—but the truth is she wanted out. She needed a change.

"I'm learning," she explained, "to stop forcing things, stop trying to meet life in a head-on crash. Nobody can wipe out his mistakes; you can only learn from them and go on from there. And so, perhaps, I have at last grown up. I'm learning to take myself as show people know how to take others, the good with the bad. I'm people, too. If I can remember that, I'll be all right."

She had that cliché word "magic" that only Jolson had.

EARL WILSON

he autumn of 1950 was a time of uncertainty. Not only for Judy Garland, but for the entire entertainment industry. All the old rules were changing: Motion picture costs were climbing, ticket sales were down, and no one knew what to expect from the little black boxes cropping up in American living rooms. MGM, which had netted $12 million in 1942, would net only $7.5 million in 1950; within a few months, Louis B. Mayer was forced into retirement. The McCarthy "red scare" was on; one performer after another was being questioned about current and past political affiliations.

Politics seemed the least of Judy's worries. "Burnt out" is the way one Hollywood columnist described her. "Little Judy Garland is probably through. Her suicide attempt was the last sputter of the self-consuming fire within her." Not everyone believed that, of course, but it would be up to Judy to prove the doomsayers wrong.

Apprehensive about her career, Judy was also concerned about the future of her marriage. She and Vincente still cared for each other very much, but, after all they had been through, Judy knew the relationship had changed. Each now had needs the other was in no position to fill.

Liza, in her own way, proved to be her mother's best medicine.

"I was able to share every day with her," Judy said later. "We became closer than we had ever been. I don't know why, but a child can bring you to believe in yourself again. Perhaps it's because of the way they believe in you. Liza helped me get some of my lost values back. She did more for me than all the psychiatrists I had been seeing for years."

Fans also lifted Judy's spirits. Letters poured in; on September 5, admirers in New York City staged what show business historians would cite as the first evidence of a "Garland cult." Judy, in town to visit friends, had stopped by Loew's Capitol to attend a performance of *Summer Stock.* On the sidewalk outside, she was met by a throng of cheering fans: "Judy! Judy! We love you!" Garland was alive and well, and her fans adored her.

Her friend Bing Crosby had also not lost faith. Judy had indirectly earned Crosby, a major stockholder in Decca Records, a sizable amount of money over the years. Bing realized this and had no intention of turning his back on the lady now. The new season of Bing's radio program was about to get under way, and he invited her to California for the first two shows.

Returning to New York, Judy starred with Thomas Mitchell in "Alice Adams," an adaptation of the Booth Tarkington story, on NBC's *United States Steel Hour.*

December brought another West Coast visit with Bing. Crosby and Garland had each been compared with one man—a performer whose talent had earned him the title of "World's Greatest Entertainer"— Al Jolson. On October 23, he had died.

In preparing their broadcast of December 6, Judy and Bing felt it appropriate to pay homage to the great master. She rummaged through Jolson's huge repertoire of hits and came up with a song she felt fit her style perfectly—"Rockabye Your Baby with a Dixie Melody." Bing's audience loved it, and Judy decided to hang on to the number.

Radio was Judy's primary medium that season, and she could not have been more pleased. There were no costumes to worry about, no cameras, no makeup. All she had to do was step in front of a microphone and sing. She let it be known that she would love to do a weekly program of her own should any net-

Judy greets her daughter Liza at the train station after Judy's visit to New York in 1950.

work be interested. Unfortunately, she was a couple of years too late. Television was already taking over, and the networks were no longer investing in new radio talent.

Movie projects continued to be discussed, but the only firm job offer came from England: producer Val Parnell renewed Lew Grade's earlier bid for Judy to appear in concert at the London Palladium. Fearful of facing such huge crowds, Judy delayed making a decision. "You've got to do it," friends advised. Judy finally instructed her agents to work out the details.

More radio work filled Judy's immediate schedule. For Christmas, *Lux Radio Theatre* staged a retelling of *The Wizard of Oz,* and in January Judy had fun with her old sparring partner on *The Bob Hope Show.* February brought another visit with Bing Crosby, a guest appearance on Tallulah Bankhead's *The Big Show,* and a *Lux* production of "Cinderella."

Judy was featured on national network television for the first time on Tuesday evening, February 27, in a CBS telecast to benefit the Red Cross. Ed Sullivan was master of ceremonies in New York; President Harry Truman spoke from Washington; featured from Hollywood were Judy, Bing Crosby, Bob Hope, and Kate Smith.

When Crosby learned Judy would be leaving soon for London, he booked her for all four of his March broadcasts. Judy took advantage of the opportunity to try out material she was thinking of including in her concerts. On March 30, Judy sailed for Europe.

A new man had entered Judy's life. His name was Michael Sidney Luft, and they had met in New York the previous fall. At home in California, they continued to date, and now the prospect of spending five weeks in London without him saddened Judy deeply.

Before sailing, Judy filed for a divorce from Vincente Minnelli. The proceedings were handled in a civilized manner, with both parties hoping to remain close friends—for Liza's sake, as well as their own.

The prospect of returning to vaudeville after a

Judy, backstage at the London Palladium, beams over white roses from her five-year-old daughter Liza in 1951.

sixteen-year absence terrified Judy. "I'm scared!" she confessed to her associates, and yet the act, she knew, was good. Roger Edens and Chuck Walters had both helped design it, and Vincente had given it his own seal of approval before she left the States.

"Her voice was better than ever," Minnelli recalled. "It had a new-found maturity. The heartache in the sad songs and the frenetic drive of the upbeat numbers created an extraordinary impact. She'd developed marvelous gestures which put the stresses on the most unexpected words. The effect was awkward and occasionally graceless, but strangely, it was right. The gestures she was developing were to become standard for other singers in a few years."

Judy's opening night was scheduled for April 8. Sid arrived the day before to surprise her, and suddenly London seemed like such a lovely place to be.

Buddy Pepper, an old friend from Judy's Lawlor days and her accompanist for the engagement, recalled that opening night as indeed something special. "The orchestra broke into the entrance music . . . Judy looked at me from the wings, terrified—and with a feeble, 'oh, no!' Then she walked on stage and it seemed as though the walls would come in with applause."

Judy sang such tunes as "Limehouse Blues," "Embraceable You," "Just One of Those Things," "Easter Parade," and the Jolson standard "Rockabye Your Baby." Midway through the evening, Pepper heard Judy finish a number, but instead of the usual audience hysteria, he heard silence. "I looked toward the mike," he recalled, "but I saw no Judy. Right behind it, however, there was our girl, flat on her you-know-what." They both let out a howl, and as he helped her back onto her feet, the audience started yelling and laughing along with them.

The evening ended with "Over the Rainbow," and, as Buddy recalled, the audience "started to roar even before she'd sung the last lyric. As the curtain folded in on the final words, 'why, oh why, can't I?' it was bedlam." "Not bad for a kid from Lancaster, California, hmm?" Judy whispered to Pepper after the last curtain call. By noon the next day, her four-week engagement was sold out.

Judy asked Sid to take over as her personal manager, and he promptly converted her Palladium booking into a two-month tour of the British Isles. Liza flew over for a visit in July, after Judy had performed in Birmingham, Blackpool, Liverpool, Dublin, Glasgow, and Edinburgh. Everywhere she played, she received the same enthusiastic response. On closing night in both Edinburgh and Dublin, the whole audience rose and sang "Auld Lang Syne," while hundreds of eager fans gathered near the footlights to wave goodbye.

"I suddenly knew that this was the beginning of a new life," Judy said. "Hollywood thought I was through; then came that wonderful opportunity . . . to appear at the London Palladium, where I can truthfully say, Judy Garland was reborn."

Judy and Sid arrived back in Manhattan on August 12, not really certain what her next project would be. Within twenty-four hours, Sid had developed a plan: Judy would bring her concert act to Broadway, to the Palace.

RKO, the owners of the Palace, thought the idea was exciting. While they redecorated the theatre, Judy and Sid rushed home to California to refurbish the act. Roger Edens and Chuck Walters both volunteered their services; so did composer Hugh Martin, who would be Judy's accompanist. Roger, now an MGM producer, restructured the Palladium rundown and added special lyrics to make the program seem more like a cohesive script-show than a disjointed concert. Chuck, long since a full-fledged director, put on his dancing shoes and worked out a series of routines for Judy and an eight-man chorus line, who were known as "Judy's Boyfriends."

Opening night had been scheduled for Tuesday, October 16; a week or so earlier Judy's whole troupe headed east on the Super Chief. They discovered the Palace had undergone a major facelift in her honor. Huge letters spelling out JUDY covered the marquee, and, inside, the whole theatre had been freshly painted. A beautiful old chandelier, salvaged from RKO's 125th Street Alhambra Theatre, was now hanging in the Palace lobby.

By the evening of October 16, Times Square was a madhouse. Thousands of fans, many without tickets, lined the streets to cheer Judy on. The crowds were so thick, Judy and Chuck Walters had to get out of their cab a block away and walk to the stage door.

At 8:40 P.M., the lights dimmed, conductor Don Albert stepped before the RKO Palace Orchestra, and the theatre's first real vaudeville program in over fifteen years was on. A series of acrobats, comedians, and dance acts were crowded into Act One.

After the intermission came the *pièce de résistance*. Judy's eight Boyfriends danced onto the stage singing a lyric Roger Edens had written ("We are here to bally-hoo . . . and to make the introductions . . ."). Eventually the boys parted, and there, hiding behind them, was Judy.

The applause threatened never to stop. Finally Judy cupped her hands to her mouth and yelled, "Hello!" This slowed the clapping, and she and the boys began "Call the Papers" and "On the Town," Edens's creations. A medley saluting the Palace and its former headliners was next; then came "Rockabye" and Judy's tribute to Jolson.

"This isn't very ladylike," Judy quipped at one point, wiping her brow with a handkerchief, "but it's very necessary."

"Gotta have some water!" she remarked later in the show. "You don't know how *hot* it is up here!" She walked over to the footlights with a pitcher and glass in her hands. "Anybody else here thirsty?"

A medley of Judy's own hits ("You Made Me Love You," "For Me and My Gal," "The Boy Next Door," and "The Trolley Song") brought another ovation; then Judy disappeared into the wings. The Boyfriends danced into view while Judy changed her clothes. When she reappeared, she was now in tights, a short tuxedo jacket, and a cocked hat. The orchestra struck up "Get Happy."

Judy dashed backstage after the number and reappeared in her tramp costume. Chuck Walters, who had trained one of the Boyfriends to dance the male part in "A Couple of Swells," insisted on performing it with Judy himself the first night.

Everyone knew there was one song still to be sung. As the applause for "Swells" died down, Judy took off her battered hat and sat down on the apron of the stage. "You've been wonderful to me tonight," she began, "and I'll never forget it. Now I want to do something special just for you—for all of you. . . ." And, there, on the edge of the stage, dressed in a ridiculous costume and lit by only a small spotlight, she sang "Over the Rainbow."

Judy revives vaudeville at its best on the stage of New York's Palace Theatre in 1951.

"There wasn't a dry eye in the Palace that night," one reporter wrote, "but there wasn't a heavy heart either. It was a happy time once again." Thunderous applause filled the theatre, and Judy took curtain calls for over ten minutes. Ushers rushed down the aisles with flowers sent from all over the world, and Judy hugged a big bouquet from Liza to her chest. "I just want to say I love you," Judy shouted, and the applause went on. . . .

Backstage was bedlam. Friends, reporters, and photographers all crushed into Judy's dressing room. Judy changed into a pale blue tulle gown and, once the din had subsided, was ready to leave for the 21 Club, where Sid had scheduled a reception.

"Don't worry," a theatre guard promised, "we'll get you out through a side door." "No, no!" Judy replied, remembering the nearly five thousand fans still gathered on the sidewalk out front. "They told me they've been waiting for over six hours. I want

to go out through the front." Out she went, arm in arm with Sid, surrounded on all four sides by policemen. Surprisingly, there was little mob disorder, only a lot of cheering.

Judy Garland and Her All Star Variety Show stayed at the Palace nineteen sold-out weeks. The original schedule of thirteen performances per week (shows at 2:40 and 8:40 daily except Monday, where there was no matinee) was grueling, and Judy was forced to miss four days in mid-November. The schedule was cut to eleven and, subsequently, to the standard eight shows per week. Closing night, February 24, 1952, was as much of a "love-in" as opening night, with the audience rising and singing "Auld Lang Syne" to a tearfully appreciative star. A few weeks later Judy received a special Tony Award for her work at the Palace.

"New York's been a great stimulant," Judy said later. "I never knew I had so many friends. With

Hugs all around as Marlene Dietrich visits Judy backstage after Garland's opening night at the Palace in 1951.

Singer Lauritz Melchior lifts Judy from the Palace stage during her closing night performance. Melchior later led the audience in serenading Judy with "Auld Lang Syne."

such encouragement, I can do anything." She insisted her "comeback," as it was now being called, had been possible only because of Sid. "He kept telling me that my career wasn't over, that it had just begun. He was so right. He took me through the dark times, and I'll never forget that."

Judy and Sid vacationed in Miami, then headed home to California. Both had gotten divorces by then—Judy from Vincente Minnelli, Sid from actress Lynn Bari—and were anxious to make plans for their future.

Sid booked *The Judy Garland Show* (as it was now called) to play four weeks at the Los Angeles Philharmonic Auditorium beginning on April 21 and another four at the Curran Theatre in San Francisco starting on May 26. But, Sid realized, one act does not a whole career make. Judy would have to tackle something else soon—preferably on the screen.

"There is one picture I'd love to do," Judy told him. "A *Star Is Born*—as a musical. I did the story on the radio once, and I wanted to do it as a picture at Metro, but they said it wouldn't be right for me." Sid quickly secured the rights.

Judy receives countless get-well wishes from fans after suffering a brief illness during her engagement at the Palace in 1951.

TONIGHT

AND FOR
FOUR WEEKS
AT THE
LOS ANGELES
PHILHARMONIC
AUDITORIUM

A special advertisement in Hollywood trade papers on April 21, 1952.

On May 21, Judy paid the first of three weekly visits to CBS Radio's *Bing Crosby Show.* For many, it seemed like old times: instead of introducing new songs, Judy and Bing concentrated on old favorites.

On June 8, while in San Francisco, Judy and Sid eloped. Now Judy discovered a wonderful secret— she was pregnant. Both parents-to-be were ecstatic.

Originally, the Lufts had discussed taking Judy's show to Dallas and Chicago during the summer. Sid considered canceling the tour and working on *A Star Is Born,* but now, with a baby on the way, he curtailed all of Judy's activities.

On June 29, the Friars Club named Judy "Miss Show Business" at a star-studded testimonial in her honor at the Biltmore Bowl in Los Angeles. "The list of celebrities who honored Judy that night is long enough to fill the Beverly Hills phone book," Homer Dickens reported later. "A stunned Judy sat tearfaced listening to each tribute that let her know she was admired and loved by her fellow professionals."

Conspicuously missing from Judy's life was Ethel. Judy and Ethel had had more mother-daughter disagreements and had gone their separate ways.

But Liza was always close at hand, as was Sid's young son, John. Judy had won custody of her daughter but agreed that the child should live six months of the year with her father. Liza later confessed to having felt bad about not being included in her mother's wedding to Sid but confirmed that everyone did his best to keep harmony in the now-extended family. Vincente later added, "Liza knew that, though her parents couldn't live together any longer, her father would always remain a Judy Garland fan."

Never too proud to accept a favor, Judy was similarly quick to offer her own services to others when a need arose. On October 25, Bing Crosby arrived

Judy closes her show at the Palace in New York.

home from a three-month trip to Europe to find his wife, Dixie Lee, dying from cancer. CBS immediately canceled Bing's scheduled broadcasts of October 30 and November 6 and began a search for replacements. Bing's brother Larry telephoned Judy with the news, and, eight months pregnant, she insisted on filling in for Bing on October 30. Bill Morrow, Bing's head writer, wrote Judy's show and later called it "the most remarkable performance I've ever seen."

On November 18, Sid escorted Judy into St. John's Hospital in Santa Monica, where, three days later, she gave birth to Lorna. Postpartum depression soon set in, so Sid got her involved in plans for *A Star Is Born*. A new family company, Transcona Enterprises, was formed, and on December 17 an alliance was struck with Warner Brothers Pictures. The deal called for nine pictures to be produced by Transcona over the next six years—three of the films to star Judy. The first of them would be *Star*. Moss Hart was commissioned to write the script, and Charles Vidor, fresh from his success with Goldwyn's *Hans Christian Andersen* (another Hart script), was a prime candidate to direct.

Judy with third husband, Sid Luft, at the Mocambo, a Hollywood nightclub, in 1952.

Judy introduces Liza to her new half-sister Lorna in 1952.

On Christmas Day, Judy, Sid, Lorna, and the baby's nurse left California on the Manhattan Limited for New York. Judy had agreed to sing at a benefit show to be staged January 5 at the Waldorf Astoria Hotel by Elsa Maxwell and the Duchess of Windsor. So as not to miss the holiday, the Lufts took a small Christmas tree, two bottles of champagne, and presents for everyone.

The holiday joy lasted less than a week into the new year. On January 5, while rehearsing for the benefit, Judy received a long-distance call from Los Angeles—her mother Ethel had died of a heart attack.

Grief-stricken, Judy told the press how sorry she was about the family rift that had estranged the two of them in recent months. "Things were straightening out between us," she said. "It's true we did have some disagreements, but we were working out a trust fund for mother and arranging to buy some property for her. But mother didn't want to depend on me."

A funeral service was held at the Little Church of the Flowers at Forest Lawn Memorial Park in Los Angeles.

Lorna, work, and good friends saved Judy from the depths of depression. Sid included her in every step of his preparations for *A Star Is Born*, and bought her a $200,000 nineteen-room mansion on Mapleton Drive in the Holmby Hills section of West Los Angeles. On the same street lived such friends as Humphrey Bogart and Lauren Bacall, Lana Turner, Art Linkletter, Sammy Cahn, and Bing Crosby.

Judy returned to *Lux Radio Theatre* one last time on February 16, for an adaptation of "Lady in the Dark," a Moss Hart play that had been made into a motion picture eight years earlier for Ginger Rogers. The intriguing and appropriate drama concerned a career woman who undergoes psychoanalysis to find the root of her problems.

Moss, meanwhile, had started work on his screenplay for *A Star Is Born*. George Cukor had replaced Charles Vidor as the man most likely to direct, and Harold Arlen and Ira Gershwin had agreed to supply the music.

On April 3, 1953, Judy walked into a recording studio for the first time in nearly six years. Mitch Miller of Columbia Records had signed her to record four songs for two new singles: "Send My Baby Back to Me," "Without a Memory," "Go Home, Joe," and "Heartbroken." Accompanied by the Paul Weston Orchestra, Judy sang the numbers some thirty times over before they had what everyone agreed were four perfect sides. The recording session lasted three hours—8 to 11 P.M. Judy, in slacks and a loose shirt to be comfortable, mussed her hair and sang to the microphone as if it were a live audience. During the playbacks, she got so nervous that she sat on the floor and hugged her knees to her chest like an excited child.

Moss Hart's screenplay for *A Star Is Born* was one of the most captivating scripts Judy had ever read. Rich in texture and scope, it included moments of comedy, drama, romance, heartache, and music. It concerned a young bandsinger (Esther Blodgett) who meets a drunken movie star (Norman Maine) at a benefit. Maine recognizes a magic in her voice and promises to turn her into a film star. He arranges a screen test, she is sensational, and the two fall in love. But with time, as her career excels, he descends further and further into a bottle until no one will hire him. When all else fails, Esther decides to abandon her career and take care of him. Norman, not wanting to destroy her life the way he had destroyed his own, quietly decides to commit suicide.

Never had Judy been handed such a script! True, she would still be playing a chorine trying to make

Ratpackers Garland and Bogart celebrate after Judy performs in Las Vegas.

it in show business, but this was about as far from "Mickey and Judy in a barn" as one could get.

James Mason had been cast as Norman; Charles Bickford, as studio chief Oliver Niles; Jack Carson, as publicity man Matt Libby; and Tommy Noonan, as Esther's friend, Danny McGuire. George Cukor directed. Rehearsals started in late summer of 1953.

"I don't like to refer to this new stage in Judy's career as a 'comeback,' " Sid told the press. "It's her first picture after a 'recess.' Judy has never been away, in any true sense of the word. The wonderful loyalty of her fans proves that. As for her health, it's excellent, probably better than that of many stars at the moment."

Production started October 12, but eight days later Warner Brothers decided they wanted to film the picture in wide-screen CinemaScope. All the completed footage had to be scrapped, and, in early November, they started over.

On a wardrobe and makeup test stage for *A Star Is Born* are (left to right) director George Cukor, cinematographer Winton Hoch, guest Mrs. Nat Lapkin, studio chief Jack L. Warner, James Mason, Judy, guest Nat Lapkin, associate executive producer Steve Trilling, and producer Sid Luft. Mr. Lapkin was an official of the Stanley Warner Theatres chain.

Judy, terrified of making another movie after so long a hiatus, worked like a Trojan—and expected everyone else to do likewise. Scenes were shot and shot again as she strove for perfection. When things

Judy is bussed by *A Star Is Born* scriptwriter Moss Hart and director George Cukor in 1953.

Warner star Doris Day visits Judy and James Mason on the set of *A Star Is Born* in 1954.

from childhood to the Palladium engagement—was in films. A musical performer loses something that way—the feel for a live audience. I'm so happy that I regained it—and a new confidence and self-assurance at the same time."

Originally budgeted at $1.8 million, the film's costs very quickly escalated—first to $3 million, then to $4 million. By the time production stretched into a fourth and fifth month, accountants were estimating a final cost of nearly $6 million.

Studio head Jack Warner refused to panic. He had seen the rushes. He knew that Judy—slowly but surely—was creating a masterpiece. Her performance was so personal, so intense, that the screen virtually crackled with excitement.

Judy also realized her work was good. "I think I've become much better," she told columnist Bob Thomas. "I know it sounds awful to say, but I never really liked myself on the screen before. But now I

went right, everyone celebrated. When they went wrong, Judy threw tantrums and barked orders at everyone within earshot. A costume designer quit after Judy screamed once too often that the clothes made her look fat (she was down to 112 pounds!), and Hugh Martin, Judy's longtime friend and musical arranger, resigned over "artistic differences." He told the press, "I thought one song ('The Man That Got Away') should be more intimate. Judy thought otherwise. To help her, I left. But I love her and am still her number one fan."

"The Man That Got Away" had special significance for Judy. She ultimately filmed it three times—in three different costumes—until the overall effect was perfect. "I love that song," she explained. "It has real drama in both words and music. It's the one I've been waiting for to introduce my 'new voice'— the 'voice' I developed by singing to those audiences at the London Palladium, the Palace in New York, and big audiences in Los Angeles and San Francisco. You see, my entire career—the important part of it,

Elizabeth Taylor and Leslie Caron visit Judy during a production break on *A Star Is Born*.

Frances Gumm, a.k.a. Judy Garland, rehearses to play Esther Blodgett, a.k.a. Vicki Lester, playing a part in a movie.

go to the rushes and I actually enjoy them. I even cry at the sad scenes. The past four years have done me a lot of good. I got out and met people and sang before live audiences. It improved my timing, and my voice is better, too. I think I look better. I don't have that 'little girl' look anymore."

The story portion of the film finished shooting February 13, and during the next couple of weeks Judy completed the last production number. Finally, the picture wrapped, and Judy and Sid drove to Ojai, California, for a much-needed vacation.

In rough-cut *Star* timed in at nearly three hours. Nowhere in the film, however, was there a number that lent evidence as to *why* Esther Blodgett became a star. Concerned, Judy called in Roger Edens, who she remembered had solved similar problems on *Presenting Lily Mars* and *Easter Parade*. As with those films, Edens suggested a showy production number— but this time not just a single number but an entire medley of familiar tunes, a showcase similar in style to those he had written for Judy to use at the Palace and the Palladium. Leonard Gershe, Edens' assistant, started work immediately on what would become a Garland landmark, "Born in a Trunk."

On June 30, *A Star Is Born* once again came to life on a Warner soundstage. Seven days were allotted to rehearsal of the new medley, nineteen more to the actual filming. Choreographer Richard Barstow directed the number, assisted by his sister, Edith,

also a choreographer. Barstow later commented, "Judy knows how much salt and pepper to put into everything. I never saw anyone who could work on so many convincing levels."

"Born in a Trunk," nearly fifteen minutes in length, pushed *Star*'s total running time past the three-hour mark. Would audiences sit that long? A preview was booked in Huntington Park (near Hollywood), and word leaked out that Judy might be there. Crowds started to form at 5:30, and by 8:30, when the film

Deleted from the original release print of *A Star Is Born* was a song within the "Born in a Trunk" medley entitled "When My Sugar Walks Down the Street."

started, there was not an empty seat in the house. The picture began, and, when Judy's name appeared on the screen, the theatre rocked with applause. It was going to be a good night!

Warner Brothers executives joined Judy and Sid at the theatre that night, and made notes on where the picture could be trimmed. The studio ultimately had a finished film with a running time of three hours and one minute.

Jack Warner, who had worried over the picture for more than a year, heaved a sigh of relief and invited the Lufts to join him on a vacation in the south of France. Judy returned home more beautiful

Judy joins Jack Warner, Debbie Reynolds, and Eddie Fisher at a birthday party for songwriter Jimmy McHugh (center) in 1954.

than ever—she was pregnant again.

On September 26, Judy joined NBC Radio's all-star tribute to Bing Crosby, a ninety-minute broadcast celebrating his twentieth year on the air. Three nights later, it was Judy's turn to be toasted: *A Star*

Judy, Marlon Brando, and Edmund O'Brien at a luncheon at which the Golden Globe Awards are announced.

Is Born premiered at the Pantages Theatre in Hollywood. Television cameras were set up in the lobby to record what columnist Earl Wilson would call "one of the greatest street carnivals in the history of mankind." Over thirty thousand people lined the sidewalks—the largest premier mob in Hollywood history—and they saw the cream of filmland royalty. Nearly every star in town came by to cheer Judy. George Jessel, acting as master of ceremonies for the evening, summed up everyone's thinking when he announced, "I happened to give Judy her name, Judith Garland, but this girl would have been great even if I'd named her Telaviv Undershirt." The celebrating continued long into the night at an after-theatre party at the Cocoanut Grove.

Life magazine called the film "a brilliantly staged, scored, and photographed film, worth all the effort." *Variety* placed it "among the top musicals . . . scoring on all counts as fine entertainment." *Motion Picture* nominated it as "1954's musical answer to *Gone with the Wind*. . . . There's no one in show

"This is Mrs. Norman Maine."

Judy holds one-year-old Joey Luft, her "personal Oscar," in 1956.

business quite like Judy Garland. Her acting adds dimension to an already unbeatable story." *Time* cited Judy's performance as "a stunning comeback," and *The Hollywood Reporter* remarked, "The entire success of the picture depends on the fact Judy really has it. . . . [One scene] ranks with the finest screen acting jobs of all time."

In October, the Lufts traveled first to New York, then to Chicago for regional premieres of *Star*. Ed Sullivan joined the celebration, including preview scenes from the film on his Sunday evening broadcast on CBS Television, October 10—the night before the film premiered in New York. Columbia Records also jumped on the bandwagon, releasing the *Star* soundtrack music in an illustrated gift box.

Everyone was talking about the picture, including theatre owners, who still considered *Star* to be too long. "Cut it!" they demanded, and Warners reluctantly agreed.

Out came nine expository scenes from the early part of the film, a song in which Norman proposes to Esther, and a major two-part production number—a total of twenty-seven minutes. George Cukor, by then directing *Bhowani Junction*, considered the

editing to be "one of the sad things of all time. . . . The picture was totally fragmented." He and Judy vowed never to view their butchered masterpiece again.

Sid, ever the entrepreneur, was already looking ahead to Judy's next movie. Richard Rodgers and Oscar Hammerstein II had two properties in which Luft had interest: *Carousel* and *South Pacific*.

Judy's name was being bantered around in connection with the upcoming Academy Awards. On February 12, the speculation ended: Judy had been nominated as Best Actress of the Year. Her competition: Grace Kelly (*The Country Girl*); Dorothy Dandridge (*Carmen Jones*); Audrey Hepburn (*Sabrina*); and Jane Wyman (*Magnificent Obsession*). "How do I feel about it?" Judy asked rhetorically. "I feel great. But I really think Grace Kelly will win. Did you see *Country Girl?* Wasn't she just wonderful in it?"

Judy was excited that *Star* had been nominated in five additional categories: Best Actor (James Mason); Best Art and Set Decoration; Best Scoring of a Musical; Best Song ("The Man That Got Away"); and Best Costume Design. Also nominated for Best

Actor was Bing Crosby (for *The Country Girl*), leading Judy to hope that if her own costar did not win, perhaps her old radio buddy would.

Excitement built during the next few weeks, especially after *Look* magazine announced its own annual movie awards: Judy and Bing were featured on a full-color cover as the "Stars of the Year."

On the evening of March 28—twenty-four hours before the Oscar telecast—Sid rushed Judy to Cedars of Lebanon Hospital. The baby was arriving prematurely. Frank Sinatra and Lauren Bacall drove to the hospital to wait with Sid, and at 2:16 A.M. on March 29, Joseph Wiley Luft was born. Bacall later recalled, "Frank had brought some kind of stuffed toy for Judy. We saw her after she came out of the recovery room, still fuzzy from the anesthesia. . . . We kissed her—Frank gave her the toy—it was a lovely moment, very sweet and thoughtful of Frank, and it meant a great deal to Judy."

The next evening Judy's hospital room looked more like a portable TV studio. NBC had sent a remote crew, just in case the clairvoyants were right, so Judy could accept her award from her bedside. Judy wanted so much to win. An Oscar would be final proof that all her work had been worth the effort, that her peers had accepted her back.

The telecast, originating a few blocks away at the Pantages Theatre, got off to a good start. Master of ceremonies Bob Hope quipped that there were mink in the audience "as far as the eye could see," and Rosemary Clooney, pinch-hitting for Judy, sang "The Man That Got Away." But as the evening progressed, things started to go wrong. One by one, the awards went to other films, other talent. Finally the big moment arrived. Bob Hope introduced presenter William Holden. Judy sat up in bed and smiled into the camera. The ominous envelope was opened—Grace Kelly!

Five minutes later, both Mason and Crosby lost when Bette Davis presented the Best Actor award to Marlon Brando.

"This is the biggest robbery since Brink's," telegraphed Groucho Marx. Even Grace Kelly's father seemed surprised. "Of course we're tickled to death with our Grace," he told the Associated Press in Philadelphia. "It's too bad they didn't have a double award so they could give one to Judy Garland."

Judy herself tried to hide her disappointment. "Grace Kelly deserved it. She did a magnificent job. After all," she said, pointing to Joey, "I was presented with my own special Oscar."

But insiders knew the hurt ran deep. As Lauren Bacall explained, with Judy "it was always all or nothing. Not winning confirmed her belief that the industry was against her. She knew it was now or never. Instinctively, all her friends knew the same."

But Judy would not stay disheartened for long. She needed applause the way most people need plasma, and if the Hollywood big shots did not want her, she knew plenty of people who did.

OVERLEAF: Portrait with hat by John Engstead, 1955.

7

She is the greatest singer of popular songs I have ever
heard, because she sings from the heart.

NOEL COWARD

If there had ever been any question about the new impor-
tance of television, the controversy had ended by 1955. In
March 1950, an estimated 4.6 million U.S. households had a
television set. Five years later, the number was 32 million. TV
was clearly here to stay, and Sid Luft wanted Judy to be a part
of it. On August 1, he and Hubbell Robinson, Jr. of CBS announced that Judy would make her long-awaited video debut on
the premiere of the new *Ford Star Jubilee* series on September
24.

The days preceding that announcement had been busy ones.
Knowing his wife's vulnerability to postpartum depression, Sid
started soon after little Joey's birth to get Judy interested in a
new career project. He launched a three-prong effort, one for
movies, one for recordings, and one for live concerts.

The Oscar snub may have hurt Judy's feelings, but it did
nothing to damage her popularity at the box office. Ticket buyers
still flocked to see *A Star Is Born*. Warner Brothers, however,
was reluctant to launch a new Garland picture until *Star* showed
a substantial profit. The Transcona contract for eight additional
films was allowed to quietly lapse.

In April, Sid worked out a long-term recording contract for
Judy with Capitol Records. Her first release would be *Miss Show*

Business, comprised primarily of material from her 1951 Palace act.

On April 19, Sid announced that Judy would spend much of July on tour. By the end of May he had put together not only a forty-person road company called *The Judy Garland Show* but also a full slate of one- and two-night engagements.

The tour opened in San Diego, California, in early July, then headed for the Pacific Northwest. The show, similar to the Palace act, had a "book" format instead of the traditional vaudeville layout—but Judy this time appeared throughout the evening. Chuck Walters staged the show, and Roger Edens supplied special musical material. Sharing the bill were the clowning Wier brothers, Jerry Gray's Or-

chestra, Frank Fontaine, the Hi-Lo's, and a dancing male chorus.

Judy loved the live audiences. Her tour of the Northwest brought back memories of playing many of the same cities with her sisters. Recalling those early days, Judy confessed, "I took one look at all those people, laughing and applauding, and I fell hopelessly in love with audiences. After all these years, I still love them, and it's been a serious romance."

In late July, *The Judy Garland Show* returned to Hollywood planning more rehearsals, then a tour of the east coast in the fall. Sid soon came up with the even more exciting plan—Judy would stage the show for television.

Initially, the idea of doing a ninety-minute live color telecast terrified Judy. It was like doing a movie, she explained, only worse—there were no retakes. "I'll just walk out there, faint dead away, and then where will I go to make a comeback?"

To alleviate her fears, Sid surrounded her with friendly people and familiar material. Much of her vaudeville act would be used, and her old pal David Wayne would be on hand to dance with Judy in "A Couple of Swells." Irene Sharaff created four new gowns for Judy; Miriam Nelson did the choreography; and Jack Cathcart—Judy's brother-in-law—directed the music.

Everything went well up to the day of the show. Then, unable to control her nerves, Judy came down with a case of laryngitis. Luckily, CBS had recorded the audio portion of Judy's numbers and could, if necessary, have her lip-sync. As it turned out, only a couple of the recordings were needed.

Judy's performance was spectacular. CBS executives were slightly unnerved by the specter of Judy dashing off stage between numbers to have her throat sprayed, never knowing if she would be able to hit a certain note or not, but the home audience sat enthralled. "Our switchboards were still jammed 24 hours after the telecast," said one CBS spokesman. "People from all over the country called just to tell us how much they liked Judy. That's all. We've never had such an intimate personal reaction from viewers before."

The *New York Times* called the show "tremen-

Judy rehearses for her video debut on *Ford Star Jubilee.*

dously appealing," and *Variety* reported, "The voice has been better, but the Garland style and the Garland heart have never been shown to better advantage. We had forgotten what gorgeous gams Judy has!"

When the ratings came in two weeks later, Ford proudly announced that their show had been seen by over twenty-five million Americans, the largest audience for a one-time-only special recorded until that date.

It was the one-time-only aspect of the show that bothered CBS the most. Judy's laryngitis had been a problem, but if she could deliver audiences like that she was well worth a few gray hairs. On October 15, CBS gave her a three-year contract (at over $80,000 per year) to star in one special every spring, starting in 1956.

Impressed by Judy's TV popularity and the size of the audiences still lining up to see *A Star Is Born*, MGM reissued *The Wizard of Oz* and, shortly there-

Judy goes over new material with pianist Leonard Pennario for her second television special in 1956.

Judy in her first television show for CBS in 1955.

after, *Meet Me in St. Louis*. Within a few months, CBS purchased the broadcast rights to *Oz* and scheduled its television premiere for the following fall.

Capitol Records had timed the release of *Miss Show Business* to coincide with the *Ford Star Jubilee* broadcast. ("See the show tonight, buy the record tomorrow," read the ads.) Both Judy and Capitol wanted to repeat the ploy with her spring telecast.

For her new album, Judy wanted to do songs she had not previously performed in public, numbers that were not identified as Garland standards. Nelson Riddle, under contract at Capitol, had given Frank Sinatra's recent recordings a more contemporary, finger-snapping beat, leaning heavily on brass and rhythm, and, although not all Judy's selections

Judy adds a new circus number to her act for her return engagement at the Palace in 1956.

would be brand new tunes, this was the sound she hoped to achieve. Riddle was hired to do Judy's arrangements, too.

The new television outing, meanwhile, would be a thirty-minute concert, scripted in part by Fred Finklehoffe. Again the idea was to get away from what Judy had done before, so fashion photographer Richard Avedon was hired to give the show a 1950s contemporary look. He decided to use stark lighting, bare stages, and "just Judy," no fancy costumes, no chorus line. Nelson Riddle was asked to do the music.

Broadcast on Sunday evening, April 8, in the time slot normally occupied by *General Electric Theater*, *The Judy Garland Show* was introduced by GE's host, Ronald Reagan. For the next half hour Judy sang. There were new songs, there were old songs, but even the old ones sounded new. None were repeats from *Ford Star Jubilee*.

As writer Randall Henderson later remarked, "If the *Ford* show had been to highlight Judy's lost, waifish side, this second effort presented her as a grown woman, in good spirits, and ready to try anything once."

Viewers were a little shocked. "What's happened to our Judy?" many complained. "Where was 'The Trolley Song,' 'You Made Me Love You,' and 'Over the Rainbow'?"

Critically a flop, *The Judy Garland Show* was a learning experience for all concerned. Judy's image was not to be tampered with. New material would have to be added from time to time, but people still expected to hear the essential Garland classics. Live television was not for Judy. Terrified throughout most of the show, she vowed "never again!" and urged Sid, "Let's use film . . . like Lucy and Desi."

Judy made her much-awaited debut in Las Vegas in late July at the New Frontier. Chuck Walters and Roger Edens were unavailable to help this time, so choreographer Robert Alton staged Judy's dances and Kay Thompson provided the special lyrics.

"Judy Makes Vegas Rafters Ring," read the headlines. "Garland the Great," explained critic Jimmy Starr, "sounds much like the billing for a stage magician—and that's very true. Judy Garland is a magician of song."

Judy's opening night gave Las Vegas its most profitable weekend since New Year's. Nearly seven thousand people were turned away, and the management quickly renewed her booking to run through Labor Day.

On September 26, Judy made her grand return to New York and the Palace Theatre. Sid, Liza, Lorna, and Joey all moved east for the occasion, and the family took an apartment in New York's Park Lane Hotel.

Opening night was not quite as boisterous as that in Vegas, but the audience loved her no less. At one point, Judy's half-slip fluttered down from beneath her black taffeta dress. "Something always has to happen to me," she said a bit bewilderedly to the audience—and from that point on she could do no wrong.

Tickets to Judy's show quickly became as hot as those to *My Fair Lady*, playing just down the street. RKO extended her booking to run indefinitely. "I'll stay a year if they'll have me," Judy promised.

With Garland, no two performances were ever exactly the same—so fans often saw her shows many times. Bing Crosby was in the audience one evening, and Judy asked him to join her in a song. Occasionally, her children would stop by, and Judy encouraged them, too, to come up on stage. When Joey was in the theatre, she would sing "Happiness Is Just a Thing Called Joe" with him in her arms. Lorna would be brought up for "Rockabye Your Baby," and Liza often joined her mother in a rousing chorus of "Swanee." Even at ten, Liza showed a penchant for toe-tapping showstoppers.

"This is all like a wonderful family party," Judy told columnist William Glover about the Palace booking. "I used to have a sort of 'I'll show 'em' attitude when I came on for a performance. Also, I used to have the most awful stage fright. Then about six months ago, I got so tired of stage fright that I tried to figure out where it came from. I said to myself, 'All those people have paid money to see you because they want to, not because somebody made them, and so they must like you.' So now, I don't want to show 'em. I just come out with a little warmth, sort of feeling like having a party."

When Glover commented that most of Judy's sixty-five-minute act was in some way related to something in Judy's private life or drawn from her movie career, she explained, "They seem to like the old songs best . . . but they like the bombastic ones, too." As for "Over the Rainbow," Judy confessed, "That's a very special song to me and my career. I still like it best of all."

Judy closed at the Palace on January 8, almost matching her nineteen-week record run in 1954. The family left at once for Los Angeles, where they promised themselves to stay put for a while. Their homecoming was marred by the death of longtime friend and neighbor, Humphrey Bogart, who had been suffering from cancer for over a year.

It was spring, time for another CBS special and a new album for Capitol. Not wanting a repeat of the 1956 fiasco, the network urged Judy to build her new special (already earmarked for Buick) around her recently completed Palace act. Judy balked, pointing out that her stage show had been culled from her whole life's work. She had already used some of the material on the 1955 *Ford* show. She could not in good conscience throw the rest of it

Judy and her singing boyfriends attract record crowds during her first Las Vegas nightclub act in 1956.

83

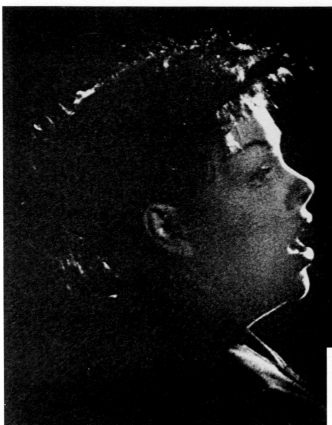

ABOVE: Judy in concert, 1956.
RIGHT: Judy at the Palace in 1956.

away on a second single television shot. What would she have left to tour with?

CBS insisted that was not their problem, and the two parties agreed to disagree. The network canceled its commitment for the special, Judy filed a breach-of-contract suit, and the dispute promised to drag on for months. Caught in the middle was Edward R. Murrow, who had planned to visit the Lufts on his weekly CBS *Person to Person* series. That program was also canceled.

Judy's new Capitol recording was called *Alone*, a potpourri of ballads about solitude. To set the mood, the jacket cover showed Judy alone on a cold, wind-swept beach. Gordon Jenkins, who had arranged many of Sinatra's brooding melodies, provided the backgrounds for the recording. Included were "By Myself," "Little Girl Blue," "Me and My Shadow," "Mean to Me," and "Among My Souvenirs." There was not a traditional Garland or Jolson song to be found.

Did this album represent a new style for Judy? "My style is really no style, because I try to sing each number differently," she explained. "I've always believed that if style takes precedent over the words and music, the audience gets cheated. It's like when people see a fine play or movie. They imagine themselves in the leading role. I want them to imagine that they're singing—not just listening to someone else." Without realizing it, Judy had explained the secret of her longevity and of the overwhelming intimacy her audiences always felt with her.

With both her picture and television careers on hold, Judy spent much of the next thirty months crossing the country and the Atlantic singing for live audiences. Her tour started May 1, 1957, with a triumphant return to Las Vegas. She was totally overwhelmed when, on opening night, the entire audience rose to its feet in the middle of "Over the Rainbow" and stood in silence while she finished.

A week's engagement followed in Detroit, where Judy sprained her ankle. She went on anyway, and fans assured her that the show was great. "Oh, sure," she smiled. "A great performance on one leg . . . but I guess stupid things like that have to happen once in a while."

Judy performed for two weeks at the Dallas Fair, where she had a chance to visit with her sister Virginia and her family, and then made her first appearance in Los Angeles in over five years at the outdoor Greek Theatre.

More traveling followed: a week in Washington, D.C., a week in Philadelphia; four weeks at the Dominion Theatre in London; then back to the Flamingo in Las Vegas.

While in London, Judy cut a new single for Capitol, "It's Lovely to Be Back in London," the song she used each night to open her act. "By Myself" was on the flip side. Judy took the English capital by storm, entertaining three thousand people nightly. Two days after she closed, she was asked to do a command performance for the royal family.

But bad things were starting to happen, too. Judy had gained much too much weight. Singing night after night left her throat raw; on more than one

occasion she came down with laryngitis. On those nights, some of the big belting numbers were dropped from the act. Rather than disappoint her fans, Judy went on and did part of the show, no matter what. Humor always saved the day. "My God!" she told one London audience. "I sound like Sophie Tucker's grandmother!"

In Las Vegas things got worse. Asked to do a New Year's Eve show, Judy—with little voice to start with—opened her act with costar Bobby Van, but found it difficult to sing above the din being made by the reveling dinner audience. When one woman tried to shout her down, Judy excused herself and canceled the balance of her engagement. Of course it was Judy, not the callous woman, who found herself in the next day's headlines.

Another incident occurred three months later at the Town and Country Club in Brooklyn. Judy completed ten nights of a three-week engagement, then quit (or was fired—depending on which story you heard) midway through a performance. "I'm sorry," she told a stunned audience, "I have terrible laryngitis. I wish I could go on, but I can't. But it doesn't matter anyhow, because I've just been fired." But Judy refused to become discouraged. She said:

I've learned that you can't run away from your problems. If that sounds corny, I apologize, but it takes a lot of learning just to get that far. I no longer expect things around me to be perfect or ever to be perfectly satisfied with myself. I used to have absurd pictures of what my life ought to be like—and when it didn't go along that way, I'd go to pieces.

But I'm past thirty-five now, and it would be tragic if I hadn't arrived at a more mature viewpoint. It's not that I'm cynical or discouraged or tired. But I've discovered that part of the wonderful richness of the world is in its imperfections.

Then, with a twinkle in her eye, Judy added, "That land that lies over the rainbow is probably a terrible bore to live in, anyhow!"

Judy started to work in earnest on two new albums for Capitol. The first, *Judy in Love*, would be a collection of romantic melodies arranged by Nelson Riddle. *Garland at the Grove*, meanwhile, would be just that: Judy's first live recording, made during her debut engagement (as an adult) at the Cocoanut Grove. The booking, she realized, was a major opportunity for her to redeem herself with anyone who had read about her troubles the previous winter. "Simply tremendous," the review read. Many critics compared her opening night to her 1951 opening at the Palace.

Judy's show, accompanied by Freddie Martin and his orchestra, was a savvy blend of traditional Garland and a few new numbers. She opened with "When You're Smiling" with special new lyrics by Roger Edens, took her audience down memory lane with "Rockabye" and "Zing! Went the Strings," which she had performed at the Grove as a child, then brought things up to date with her own special rendition of a 1958 nonsense song, "The Purple People Eater." "Rainbow," of course, closed the show.

Judy's triumph at the Grove was followed by similar performances at Orchestra Hall in Chicago, the Sands in Las Vegas, and the Fontainebleau in Miami Beach.

Judy in Love was released to stores in November, and *Garland at the Grove* the following February. In the interim, Judy started work on perhaps the most innovative album of her career, *The Letter*. Telling a love story set to music, the album introduced such songs as "The Worst Kind of Man," "That's All There Is, There Isn't Any More," and "The Red Balloon." Actor John Ireland appeared on the disc as Judy's lover, and they were backed by the Ralph Brewster Singers, and Gordon Jenkins and his orchestra.

On May 11, Judy went highbrow—sort of. She opened a new act at the Metropolitan Opera House in New York, with a percentage of the proceeds to go to a children's charity. Judy's vaudeville show was the first nonclassical entertainment to play the Metropolitan since the 1920s, when Scottish comedian Sir Harry Lauder filled the rafters with humor. "Why the Met?" one columnist asked the now very rotund Garland. "What's the matter?" she retorted with a smile, "Don't you think I have the figure for it?"

Her act, previewed two weeks earlier in Baltimore, included dancer John Bubbles, comedian Alan King, a company of sixteen singers and fourteen dancers, and conductor Gordon Jenkins. Chuck Walters staged the show; Roger Edens supplied special material; Richard Barstow did the choreography; and Irene Sharaff designed the costumes and scenery.

"Judy Garland Rocks the Met for Charity," announced the headlines, and first-nighters—who paid up to $500 each for seats—kept her on stage for fourteen curtain calls.

The engagement lasted seven nights, after which Sid booked the show to play a week each at the Chicago Civic Opera, the San Francisco Opera, and the Los Angeles Shrine Auditorium.

When the tour ended, Judy wanted only to rest. By casual estimate, she had done nearly three hundred live performances during the past three years, and

Judy wows 'em at the Cocoanut Grove in 1958.

all the traveling had taken its toll. She was grossly overweight and was feeling awful.

Concerned about her weight, Sid suggested she visit a health farm. To make it sound more agreeable, he decided to make an adventure out of it—the whole family would go. Liza lost fifteen pounds on a cheese and carrots diet; Sid lost ten; Judy lost nothing. Physically and emotionally she felt worse than ever. Sid knew it was time for serious action.

A week before Thanksgiving, the Lufts flew to New York. Judy was admitted to Doctors Hospital; the diagnosis was a diseased liver. The many years of diet pills, pep pills, alcohol, poor nutrition, late hours, and working herself to a frazzle had left her body a wreck.

For the next few weeks Judy's prognosis was touch and go. Sid often spent the night at the hospital. The doctors warned that her health didn't look good.

Get-well cards, flowers, and, ultimately, Christmas gifts descended on the hospital from all over the world. For over a month, Judy lay flat on her back, totally dependent on those around her. Finally, by Christmas, she was able to sit up. A fan club based in the midwest sent her a copy of James Michener's *Hawaii*, and she was so tired of staring at the ceiling that she read most of it in one day. Her condition continued to improve, and on Tuesday, January 5, her physicians allowed her to leave.

She was still a very sick woman. To the press, Judy called it hepatitis—even though a few cynics speculated about cirrhosis. Either way, doctors warned that she would be a semi-invalid and that she would never be able to work again. Judy shared all these details with the press. What she did not reveal was that her doctors had privately predicted that, although she was only thirty-seven, she had only five more years to live.

Judy left the hospital with only one thought in mind—home. The Lufts took a cab directly to the train station and, after a brief stop in Chicago, headed straight for Los Angeles. Judy was determined to get there by the weekend. Liza was making a solo appearance on Hedda Hopper's local television show, and, now more than ever, Judy wanted to see it.

OVERLEAF: Judy, as Jenny Bowman, entertains at the London Palladium in *I Could Go On Singing*, 1962.

8

A Garland audience doesn't just listen, they feel.
They have their arms around her when she works.
SPENCER TRACY

"When the doctor told me that work was out of the question," Judy confessed later, "I didn't care . . . I just didn't care. The pressure was off me for the first time in my life. All I cared about was being with the children. I lay there, watched TV, read novels, and thought, 'No more pills, ever.' "

The love that was shown to Judy had immediate results. She regained her health; she began to lose weight slowly, then started to feel good about herself for the first time in years. There were days when she said, with honesty, "I have no ambition to be an actress, no ambition to be a singer, I have absolutely no drive. . . . I just want to be a mother."

But there were also days when the children were at school, when there was nothing interesting to read or watch on television, when the old adrenalin started to flow.

In April, Judy made the first step toward reviving her career. George Sidney, her director on *The Harvey Girls*, was preparing an all-star picture at Columbia, *Pepe*. No, he did not want her to appear—he wanted her to sing on the soundtrack. That sounded simple enough, and in a matter of hours, Judy had rehearsed and recorded Andre Previn's beautiful "Far Away Part of Town."

A visit to Capitol Records was next. Together with conductor Jack Marshall, she selected twelve songs—a few for orchestra

Judy checks her makeup for the opening night at the London Palladium in 1957.

Judy lends her support to the annual March of Dimes campaign.

accompaniment, some just for piano or guitar. *Judy: That's Entertainment!* was designed to demonstrate once again the versatility of the Garland voice.

Judy started to see friends again. Peter Lawford, her buddy from *Easter Parade*, and his wife Patricia invited the Lufts to a dinner party they were hosting at their Santa Monica home in early July. Patricia's family was in town that week for the Democratic National Convention; her brother John Kennedy hoped to be nominated for the presidency.

On Sunday evening, July 10, Judy, Frank Sinatra, Sammy Davis, Jr., and Mort Sahl provided the entertainment for the convention's opening banquet. Earl Wilson later reported, "Frank and Judy were the most ogled names at the dinner and the biggest stars . . . Judy was the belle of the party." Photographs were taken that night, and Judy carried a wallet-size picture of her and JFK in her purse the rest of her life.

By the time the senator was officially nominated by his party, Judy was in London. She was there for recording sessions with orchestra leader Norrie Paramor, but the enthusiastic reception she received discouraged her from hurrying home.

"When I arrived," Judy told the press, "I was so impressed by the tempo, people, atmosphere and cordiality that I phoned my husband and said, 'Why don't we all move to England?' He was delighted."

Beginning Tuesday, August 2, Judy locked herself away at the Capitol/EMI studios and, over the next eight days, recorded eighteen songs and two medleys in beautiful new "stereophonic" sound.

"Judy sounded remarkably happy at this stage in her life," Norrie Paramor recalled later. "She always had a great sense of humor and she was certainly at the top of her form with us."

Capitol elected not to release the recordings immediately; in fact, they kept most of them in their vaults until after Judy's death, when they were issued on an album called *Judy in London*. But the EMI sessions were not for naught—they sparked Judy's enthusiasm and provided an excellent inventory of material for a new one-woman show. Opening night was scheduled for August 28 at one of Judy's favorite places, the London Palladium.

"Judy Packs Pep!" wrote Jack Bentley in the *Sunday Pictorial*, and, indeed, Judy's performance at the Palladium firmly reestablished her credibility as an entertainer. Playwright Edward Albee found the evening "superb." Judy admitted, "It was a pistol!" A second performance was quickly scheduled for Sunday, September 4, and was also a hit.

The Lufts took a five-month lease on a large home owned by Sir Carol Reed in Chelsea. Sid put the Holmby Hills house up for sale, the children arrived from the United States, and even Fred Finklehoffe came to coauthor Judy's life story. The book never materialized.

On October 5, Judy made the first of two appearances in Paris, doing her one-woman show for capacity crowds at the Palais de Chaillot auditorium. More concerts were scheduled, two at the Olympia in Paris, another in Amsterdam.

Judy had another mission that fall—helping her friend John Kennedy get elected president of the United States. All of Peter Lawford's Hollywood friends had volunteered, and Judy wanted to do her part, too. The Kennedy campaign named Judy their "European representative," and so she gave two free concerts at U.S. military bases in Germany, to make sure citizens posted their votes by the November 3 deadline.

"I've known the Kennedy family for a long time," she told the press proudly. "I'm a great fan of Jack's, and I hope he's a fan of mine. I have a great belief in him. He's wonderful, warm, human, and imaginative. That's the message I'm going to give as many American citizens as I can find in Europe."

Judy was particularly pleased when, on November 8, 1960, John F. Kennedy was elected by one of the slimmest popular-vote margins in history.

In January, Judy did a one-night-stand at the huge Deauville Hotel in Miami to compensate for an appearance she had had to cancel a year earlier. The Lufts confessed that they were all migrating back to the United States, at least temporarily.

Sid arranged for Freddie Fields and Freddie Fields Associates to take over as Judy's agents. Fields outlined wonderful plans for her. "If you want to weigh 140 or 150, fine," he promised. "I'll get you the best 150-pound parts—because you're the best 150 pounds in the business."

True to his word, Fields quickly settled Judy's four-year legal hassle with CBS and began negotiations for a new television special. He initiated talks for a small but dynamic role in Stanley Kramer's new film, *Judgment at Nuremberg* and booked Judy's one-woman show for a six-week, fourteen-city tour.

"With Freddie," Judy admitted, "something clicked. He seemed to know how to do exactly what I can't do: channel my work."

But things at home had hit a snag. In January, as Judy prepared for her tour, she asked Sid for a sep-

aration. She needed some time to be on her own, she explained. Sid was shocked at the notion, and for the next twelve months they vacillated between living together and living apart, reconciling and breaking up all over again.

Stanley Kramer welcomed Judy to *Judgment at Nuremberg* with open arms. The role was that of a German housewife who is asked to testify against the accused Nazi judges who, years earlier, had ordered the execution of her friend, a prominent Jewish citizen. There was no singing involved, but the script required Judy to become emotional and to break down in tears while on the witness stand.

Starring in the film were Spencer Tracy, Burt Lancaster, Richard Widmark, Marlene Dietrich, Maximilian Schell, and Montgomery Clift.

Upon arriving on the set of Stage 9 at Universal Studios in early March, Judy was greeted with applause from cast and crew. She had only words of praise for director Kramer: "He never looked at me

Judy campaigns for John F. Kennedy at a Democratic rally in Wiesbaden, Germany, in 1960.

with a doubtful look and never asked questions about me. He treated me as a working actress. This was the final vote of confidence I needed."

Once Judy's three scenes were completed, she flew back to London to look for a house. Producers Stuart Millar and Lawrence Turman had interested both Judy and actor Dirk Bogarde in a Bob Dozier story idea, *The Lonely Stage.* If the contracts and financing could be worked out, the picture would be filmed over the summer.

"I'll be Dirk Bogarde's houseguest this quick trip," Judy told Louella Parsons, "because I'm due back in New York April 6 for some concert dates and my Carnegie Hall appearance April 23."

Judy was unable to satisfy her real estate problem that spring, but on April 6 in Buffalo she resumed her concerts. Dates in Washington, D.C., Birmingham, Atlanta, Charlotte, and Greensboro followed on an every-other-night basis, and on April 23 she was responsible for what many observers considered to be "the most memorable night in show business history." New York's Carnegie Hall was filled to capacity—everyone from shoe clerks to entertainment royalty had come to cheer. Early arrivals included Rock Hudson, Lauren Bacall, Jason Robards, Henry Fonda, Julie Andrews, Richard Burton, Carol Channing, Phil Silvers, and Harold Arlen.

Waiting backstage, Judy was petrified. "I kept thinking of who was out front—and I kept telling myself, 'This ain't Dallas, kiddo! This is Carnegie

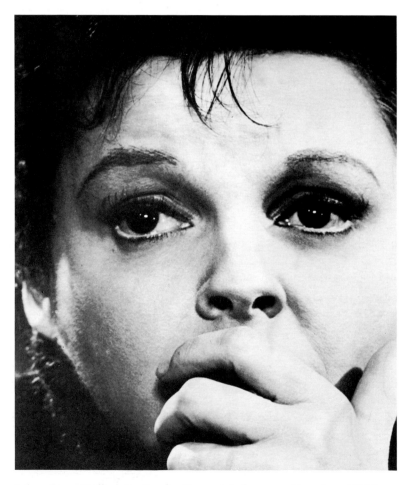

Judy as Irene Hoffman in Stanley Kramer's *Judgment at Nuremberg* (1961).

The living legend greets her admirers after a stunning performance at New York's Carnegie Hall in 1961.

Hall, New York City—and I ain't Heifetz or Rubinstein!' "

Indeed, no. But this audience had come to hear Garland. As she stepped out onto the stage, the response was deafening—not just applause, but screams, squeals, and shouts of adulation. There were so many open mouths, Kay Thompson recalled later, that "the whole front row looked like a dentist's ad!"

"I decided right away," remembered Judy, "that they liked me and I loved them, and we had ourselves a ball!"

For nearly three hours Judy could do no wrong. She ripped through nearly every song she had ever known, bringing first a smile to the audience's face, then a tap to the foot, a lump to the throat, and a tear to the eye.

"Nothing in show business will ever touch it," Merv Griffin said. "No Broadway opening, film premiere, nothing. Garland—performer and legend were one that night, and magic. All New York turned out to see her, and Judy left us standing on our chairs, weeping and cheering and totally drained."

Hedda Hopper agreed: "Judy Garland took a jam-packed crowd in Carnegie Hall in her arms and they hugged her right back—never saw the like in my life. We laughed, cried, and split our gloves applauding. A standing ovation on her entrance lasted four minutes. Each song got thunderous applause and at least half a dozen times the audience rose in appreciation."

Capitol Records, sensing history in the making, had wisely recorded the performance on a new album. The evening was so successful that Freddie Fields booked *Another Evening at Carnegie Hall* for May 21. In the interim, there were concerts in Philadelphia and the Chicago Opera House.

Negotiations for *The Lonely Stage* continued, but when Millar and Turman postponed production until the following spring, Judy decided she would spend the summer in the United States. Ted Kennedy invited her to rent a house in Hyannis Port, Massachusetts, and spend July and August with "the family." Judy did one concert on July 1 at the Forest Hills Tennis Club in New York and another on July 3 at the Music at Newport Festival in Rhode Island, and then drove to Cape Cod to join her children.

The great thing about the Kennedy clan, Judy realized, was the number of youngsters in the com-

Burt Lancaster entertains Judy and director John Cassavetes between scenes of the somber A Child Is Waiting.

bined families. It promised to be, in her words, "the best kind of summer Joey and Lorna could have had—sailing, swimming, even tennis lessons."

Liza, now fifteen, kept herself busy working sixteen hours a day, six days a week, as an apprentice at the Cape Cod Melody Tent summer theatre. Richard Brock, a member of the chorus that summer, recalled Judy taking an avid interest in Liza's work: "Judy would attend our performances and even invite us back to her house for after-theatre celebrations. One afternoon both Judy and Jackie Kennedy came to a show, and, I think, Judy drew the most attention. The thing I remember most, however, is the genuine affection Judy had for her children, and vice versa. They really cared for one another."

Vincente Minnelli stopped in Hyannis Port to see Liza perform in Take Me Along at the Melody Tent, but Sid Luft was nowhere to be found. "We reconciled several times," Judy confessed, "but it didn't work out. I have no plans to file for a divorce. We are perfectly friendly, and he calls the children two or three times a week."

Judy at Carnegie Hall, an expensive ($10) two-record set, was issued by Capitol in late July; within a few weeks it had sold over one hundred thousand copies. The album won five Grammy Awards and is one of the biggest-selling recordings of all time.

Clearly in demand, Judy interrupted her summer for a return engagement at Forest Hills. As Labor Day approached, she prepared to start her cross-country tour again. She rented a house in Scarsdale, New York, to use as home base, then started off to San Francisco, Los Angeles, Denver, Boston, Montreal, Newark, Pittsburgh, Miami, Atlantic City, White Plains, and Rochester.

Between concerts, she entertained at a charity benefit in Los Angeles and provided the voice of Mewsett, a cat, in a feature-length animated feature, Gay Purr-ee. The highlight of this assignment was singing four new songs by old friends Harold Arlen and Yip Harburg.

Judy's appearance at the Hollywood Bowl on September 16 was perhaps the most memorable of Judy's autumn concert dates. She performed in the rain. Over twenty thousand fans jammed the Bowl—a record—and even though it started to drizzle, no one moved. "They put up umbrellas and pulled coats over their heads," Freddie Fields later reported, "but not one of them left. They even made her sing 'San Francisco' again, after 'Chicago.' "

Finally, the last city had been visited, the last song sung, the last bag unpacked. "This is the first time I've ever felt a sense of accomplishment," Judy

94

told an interviewer. "I'm free now. For a few days, even my voice is my own. I feel like sitting in a draft in a wet bathing suit!"

By Christmas Judy and Sid had patched up their differences—at least temporarily—and the family spent a peaceful holiday in Scarsdale. For New Year's, the Lufts flew to Los Angeles, where Judy started rehearsing her first television special in six years.

The Judy Garland Show, as the program was called, had Frank Sinatra and Dean Martin as guests and was taped at CBS Television City over a period of three nights. Norman Jewison produced and directed; Kay Thompson served as creative consultant.

"I never liked TV," Judy confessed. "It scared me until now." But having Sinatra and Martin on hand certainly provided moral support. "It's the first time we have ever worked together," she said, "and it was Dean and Frank who made it exciting. They were marvelous. . . . There's no need for weeks of rehearsal if you have good people around. Most of the show is the three of us singing—and we knew the songs!"

CBS scheduled the show to air Sunday, February 25, in its most competitive time slot—opposite NBC's top-rated western, *Bonanza.* Over twelve and a half

million homes (twenty-five million viewers) tuned in to watch. CBS promptly scheduled a rerun for September 19. Cecil Smith of the *Los Angeles Times* called the hour "as memorable as any television has ever given us."

"It's a great thing to lose fear," Judy said. "I had an unreasonable block against television, and I had to break through this final block in my life. My previous TV shows were utter chaos to me because I was so frightened."

Judy's interest in psychology and her keen respect for Stanley Kramer led to her next engagement, the role of a music teacher in a school for mentally retarded children in Kramer's new film, *A Child Is Waiting.* Burt Lancaster costarred, along with Gena Rowlands and Steven Hill. Rowlands' husband, John Cassavetes, directed.

It was during the production of *A Child Is Waiting* that the Motion Picture Academy nominated Judy for Best Supporting Actress for her work in *Judgment at Nuremberg.* "I *never* win awards," she told columnist Sheilah Graham. Indeed, the trophy that year went to Rita Moreno for *West Side Story.*

That spring Capitol released *The Garland Touch,* a play on the title *The Garlund Touch,* a current

Dean Martin and Frank Sinatra turn Judy's third television special into a relaxed hour of music in 1962.

television private eye series. Included were several of the tracks Judy had recorded in London with Norrie Paramor, as well as two songs with Mort Lindsey and his orchestra issued as a single the previous autumn.

On April 26 a new album of show tunes, *Judy Takes Broadway,* was started in New York. With the exception of "Just in Time" and "Never Will I Marry," all the songs were new to the Garland repertoire: "Sail Away," "Something's Coming," "Get Me to the Church on Time," "Joey, Joey," "Hey, Look Me Over," "76 Trombones," "Why Can't I Do What You Do?" "The Party's Over," and "Some People." These numbers were recorded live at the Manhattan Center before an audience of celebrities and enthusiastic fans. Judy started the late-night session at midnight and sang into the small hours of the morning. The resulting tapes were not considered quite good enough, and would remain unreleased for another fifteen years.

The Wizard of Oz songwriters also provided music for Judy's last film, *I Could Go On Singing* (1962).

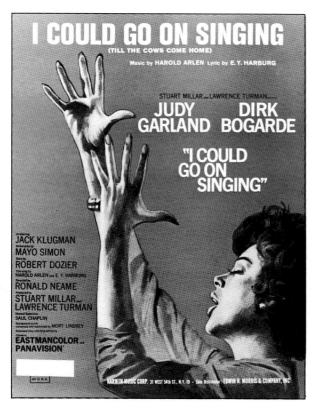

Judy's Las Vegas act, like her old movies on television, plays to early morning audiences (1962).

On April 28, she flew to London to film *The Lonely Stage,* soon to be retitled *I Could Go On Singing.* A musical drama, the picture told the story of a very Judy-like concert artist, Jenny Bowman. While appearing at the Palladium, Jenny visits the English surgeon who had fathered—and now has custody of—her only child. She gave up the boy to pursue her career, and now, having reached the top and found "the applause empty and the stage lonely," she attempts to reclaim both the physician and their son. Bogarde portrayed the surgeon; Gregory Phillips, the child; Jack Klugman, her manager; and Aline MacMahon, her dresser and confidante.

Director Ronald Neame arranged to shoot scenes at many famous English landmarks and rented the Palladium for shots of Jenny (Judy) on stage. Over a thousand extra players were paid to sit and listen to Judy sing for several days. Songs included "I Could Go on Singing" and "Hello Bluebird." Judy invited nearly a hundred members of her English fan club to see her in action. Their affectionate bursts of applause were not in the script but lent just the right touch of authenticity to the scenes. The last day of shooting was perhaps the best. As Judy strutted down the runway belting out her final number, the crowd went mad. "It was like a real first night," Judy said later. "I finally had to hold my arms out to that paid audience and try to express my gratitude."

I Could Go On Singing wrapped in early August, and Judy and the children headed back to the States where, a month later, she started a four-week engagement at the Sahara Hotel in Las Vegas. Opening night was standing room only, and for over an hour Judy entertained an audience that included Ray Bolger, Spike Jones, Ed Sullivan, George Burns, Henry Fonda, Carol Channing, and Carol Burnett.

At the end of Judy's four weeks, the management invited her to stay on for another two. She agreed, but she asked for one major change: for the first month, she had appeared once nightly at the dinner show and Ray Bolger had come on at midnight. For the new engagement, Judy wanted to appear once nightly—at 2:30 A.M.!

One morning after Judy's late-night show, she donated her talent to the creation of a made-for-disc musical comedy, *Three Billion Millionaires*, on behalf of the U.S. Committee to the United Nations.

Judy's relationship with Sid hit an all-time low that autumn. Each sued the other for a divorce and custody of the children. By February, they had kissed and made up.

Gay Purr-ee opened in theatres in November, and, on December 7 Judy made her first network television guest appearance on *The Jack Paar Show* to plug the picture. Judy demonstrated her abilities as storyteller, sharing anecdotes about the Gumm Sisters and *The Wizard of Oz*. From her new picture she sang "Little Drops of Rain," "Paris Is a Lonely Town," and, with fellow-guest Robert Goulet, "Mewsette."

Judy's success on the *Paar Show* on NBC caught everyone's attention, especially those at CBS who were preparing a new special for her to air in the spring. They were particularly pleased by Judy's easygoing demeanor and abilities as a raconteur. On December 28, CBS announced that it had booked Goulet and Phil Silvers for her special; three days later, on New Year's Eve, the network revealed that Judy had agreed to star in a sixty-minute weekly variety series to premiere in the fall.

Suddenly, 1963 promised to be a very interesting year.

Judy reveals her talents as a raconteur on Jack Paar's television program in 1962.

OVERLEAF: Judy by John Engstead.

9

Judy Garland is the only giant left in the industry. She is the only one with a legend attached to everything she does. There's a magical quality about her.

GEORGE SCHLATTER

"The Great Garland Gamble" is the way *TV Guide* heralded Judy's new love affair with the video medium. There was nothing riskier than a television series. Every year dozens of new programs were announced, and only a very small percentage proved successful. To fail meant to do so in full view of the whole country; to succeed meant untold riches and the adoration of millions.

Judy Garland and Her Guests Phil Silvers and Robert Goulet (the rather cumbersome title of her special) was taped in New York in January 1963. Burt Shevelove produced, Charles Dubin directed, Larry Gelbart wrote the script, and Mort Lindsey served as musical director. The special, announced as a "preview/pilot" of Judy's new fall series, aired March 19, attracting an estimated audience of over twenty-two million people. A few critics carped about the sets, others questioned the need for Judy to do anything but sing, but few could deny the program's overall success.

A Child Is Waiting opened that winter to mixed reviews and so-so business. "This film about retarded children," wrote one critic, "is deeply touching and instructive, but a spectator who is not immediately concerned with this particular problem may find that constant sadness a little too much. Burt Lancaster, as a tough-minded doctor who fights to gain human dignity for the

TOP LEFT: Phil Silvers, Judy (in Phil's beard), and Robert Goulet poke fun at folksingers in her fourth television special in 1963.

TOP RIGHT: Judy rehearses with Count Basie in 1963.

BOTTOM LEFT: "I love this girl," says Mickey Rooney during rehearsals with Judy in 1963. "I've always loved her."

BOTTOM RIGHT: Judy and Lena Horne do a medley of songs they made famous on a segment of *The Judy Garland Show* in 1963.

defective youngsters, and Judy Garland, as a lost woman who wants to help, are both excellent." Director John Cassavetes was similarly praised for giving the film a semidocumentary style, but, as *Films in Review* magazine warned, the commercial problems of the picture proved "insuperable."

I Could Go On Singing followed *Child* into the theatres. On March 4, Judy flew to London for its world premiere. A crowd mobbed her as she arrived in Piccadilly Circus, and, inside the Plaza Theatre, the audience gave her a standing ovation. At a post-premiere party, Judy was toasted by nearly every big name in English filmmaking.

On March 10, Judy appeared on the English television series *Sunday Night at the London Palladium.* She sang a medley of songs and plugged her new picture. Twice, she missed a song cue. Humor again came to her rescue, when she held her arms up and told the orchestra, "Come on, now, let's stop! We can even stop on television, yes we can—I can make just as many mistakes!" The audience laughed with her, and the rest of the show proceeded smoothly. "Gee, it's ridiculous," she confessed later. "I've sung that song 'live' scores of times. I recorded it, and every time without a hitch."

Judy donated her salary—the highest ever paid on the *Palladium* television program—to Lady Hoare's Fund to Aid Thalidomide Children. The money went to buy artificial arms and legs for the afflicted youngsters.

I Could Go On Singing received only lukewarm reviews in England, but the critics loved Judy. "I can't think of one artist who could give so much to so little," wrote Fergus Cashin of the London *Daily Sketch.* "Judy stands out in this awful corn like a poppy. She's a good actress, all she needs is a good film. I hope she gets one soon."

Ed Sullivan saluted the picture and the star on his program of April 14, produced entirely in London. Included was footage of the Plaza premiere and tape from Judy's performance on the *Palladium* show.

Meanwhile, preparations were underway for CBS's new *Judy Garland Show.* George Schlatter, producer of many Dinah Shore programs and Andy Williams specials, was hired to head the new series, with assistance from scenic designer Gary Smith, associate producer. Bill Hobin, veteran of various television

musical series, would direct. Singer-composer Mel Torme came on board to supply vocal routines and special musical material, and Jerry Van Dyke was chosen to serve as resident funnyman and sometime kibitzer, much as Judy had once heckled Bob Hope.

The Judy Garland Show, like her most recent special, was originally conceived as a New York-based production. Because of Manhattan's oppressively hot summers and CBS's more lavish facilities in California, Schlatter and company decided to ensconce themselves at CBS Television City in Hollywood.

Judy put a down payment on a beautiful new home on Rockingham Drive in Brentwood, and CBS showed her the royal treatment at the studio. A charming yellow-brick road was painted on the walkway between Stage 43 and the door of a new, candy-striped dressing room trailer that had been decorated especially for Judy. The stage was raised, a special revolving turntable embedded in the floor, and theatre seats were installed to make the room look like a concert stage.

Judy's opening night taping was scheduled for Monday, June 24. For her first guest, Judy requested Mickey Rooney. "I can't do the first one with anyone but Mickey," she told Schlatter. "He's my partner. He'll put me at ease, and he'll be damn good for the show." The audience would also be special that night—only family, friends, network executives, and nearly every big-name star on the CBS schedule.

Mickey and Judy went through their paces, singing "You're So Right for Me," reminiscing about MGM, and recreating Mickey's "Tournament Golfer" pantomime routine. Judy closed the show with a stirring rendition of "Old Man River."

"It was the most nostalgic thing Judy's done since she sang the love letter to Mr. Gable," wrote Hedda Hopper. "Watching Garland and Rooney sing, clown, ad lib and dance took you right back to the old Andy Hardy days, when she first fell under his spell."

Four more programs were taped in close succession: one with Count Basie on July 7; Liza Minnelli, in her first professional appearance with Judy, on July 16; Lena Horne and Terry Thomas on July 23; and Tony Bennett on July 30. Suddenly, on August 5, nearly half of the creative staff was fired.

CBS was unhappy because it felt that the programs looked more like individual specials than episodes of a continuing series. Schlatter and three writers were pink-slipped. Big-name guests, the network felt, were not as important as recognizable *television* talent. "Any weekly show has to be formatted," a network spokesman said. "There have to be standard compartments that audiences look forward to."

CBS wanted to change Judy's image from that of a sophisticated chanteuse to that of "the girl next door." Test audiences found her too aloof, too unreachable. The network also noticed that Judy—perhaps out of nervousness—was touching her guests too much.

The network's logic may or may not have had merit, but the sudden dismissal of Judy's staff undermined her confidence. Already jousting with Sid again, in a few short weeks Judy had come to rely on her television team for emotional support. Now all the faces were changing. Norman Jewison, who had produced Judy's 1962 special, was brought in as executive producer; Gary Smith was promoted to producer; and a battery of writers were hired to develop the "new" Garland image.

Scripts were now carefully formatted . . . an opening number, a comedy bit for Van Dyke, a number with a guest, etc. A new "talk fest," in which Judy and her guest sipped tea and chatted, became a weekly feature, as had Schlatter's idea of closing with Judy on a runway rummaging through an old wardrobe trunk. The "Born in a Trunk" feature led automatically into one or two closing numbers, then into Judy's closing theme, "I Will Come Back."

June Allyson and Steve Lawrence were guests on the first new show, taped September 13. The women reminisced about their MGM experiences and sang together for the first time. Donald O'Connor guest-starred the following week; that show also became a trip down memory lane. CBS and Jewison were determined to make this program the series opener, even though publicity had been out for weeks that the Rooney show would be up first. The switch may have confused a few viewers, but the O'Connor show delighted millions. President Kennedy sent Judy a wire: "Congratulations on a wonderful show. . . . Know it will be a big hit in the coming season."

"Miss Garland worked a wizard's spell," said the *New York Herald Tribune*. "It was a bright, engaging show," agreed the *New York Telegraph & Sun*, "sur-

Judy joins other show business mothers in protesting children killed in the bombing of a Birmingham, Alabama, church. Left to right: Carolyn Jones, June Allyson, Pamela Powell (June's daughter), Liza Minnelli, and Judy (1963).

Judy and Donald O'Connor prepare for the premiere of Judy's television series in 1963.

prises opening out of surprises." Columnist Ben Gross of the *New York Daily News* elaborated: "especially pleasing was Judy's get-together with Don, who proved himself to be an ideal guest. Their revival of forgotten vaudeville numbers, their song-studded reminiscences of childhood days, and, above all, their performance of 'The Old Soft Shoe' were endearing."

Another episode, in which the Smothers Brothers and the new hit of Broadway, young Barbra Streisand, were guests, was taped on Friday, October 4. It also proved too irresistible to save, and was rushed on the air with very little promotion on October 6. It was an excellent second show.

Satisfying CBS's request that contemporary television talent be booked as guests, Jewison loaded other segments with George Maharis, the Dillards, Steve Allen, Zina Bethune (then starring on the network's *The Nurses* series), and comedian Jack Carter. Ray Bolger stopped by for another evening of nostalgia, and Peggy Lee joined Judy for an hour of serious harmonizing.

Unfortunately, in 1963, television did not care as much about quality as it did about quantity—and

when the first national Nielsen survey of the season was released, it indicated *The Judy Garland Show* had been soundly thrashed by *Bonanza* on NBC.

The star was both confused and betrayed. "Judy just seemed unhappy because she didn't quite understand what was going on," Jewison said. Schlatter's team had told her she was "just marvelous, the show is wonderful," yet the network had ordered changes. Jewison made the changes, yet no one was watching.

"I don't think *I'd* look at my show every week," Judy confessed. "It's too enervating. I think it should be a bit easier for people to watch. We're in trouble if we can't calm down a bit."

Although the unexpected summer hiatus had eaten up much of the slack time in the schedule, a week's production break was called in late October. Judy flew to New York for meetings with top network officials.

Norman Jewison's commitment for eight shows, and Bill Hobin's for thirteen, were about to end, and both men had resigned. While in New York, Judy hired William Colleran, producer of several Frank Sinatra and Bing Crosby specials, to replace

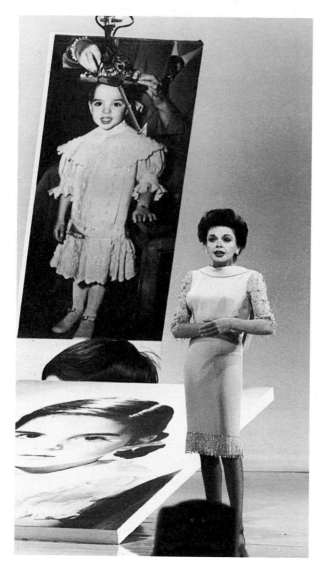

In 1963, Judy introduces Liza Minnelli on her television series with photos from the past—*In the Good Old Summertime* (1949).

program to the fallen leader. She suggested a concert of patriotic songs—everything from "Keep the Home Fires Burning" to "America the Beautiful"—but CBS said no. "The whole country has been in mourning for four days," network president James Aubrey pointed out. From now on, he wanted escapist programming as usual.

Judy was heartbroken but lost herself in a special Christmas program scheduled to be taped December 6. A set had been built to simulate Judy's home, and invited guests would include Liza, Lorna, and Joey. Jack Jones would be "stopping by" to sing a few songs, as would Mel Torme. Judy finally relented and sang "Over the Rainbow" for the first time on television since 1955.

The next week, Judy found a way to outsmart Aubrey. If she could not do a show for President Kennedy, she could at least do one song. For her closing number, slipped surreptitiously to Mort Lindsey earlier in the week, Judy stood out on the darkened stage, stared into the spotlight, and sang "The Battle Hymn of the Republic"—and sang it as it had never been sung before. "The emotion in the studio at that moment was purer than Ivory soap,"

Judy gets physical with handsome guest George Maharis in 1963.

Jewison, and Dean Whitmore, director of *The Dinah Shore Show* to replace Hobin. Jerry Van Dyke had also resigned and was not replaced.

Judy returned to Los Angeles, taped a couple more shows, then started a prearranged two-week Thanksgiving holiday.

On Friday, November 22, while planning a small birthday gathering for Lorna, Judy turned on the radio—and stopped cold in her tracks. The news was too much to bear. Her friend Jack Kennedy had been killed in Dallas.

Seldom did Judy insist on doing a certain number on her series, but the Kennedy assassination left her stunned, and she wanted to dedicate her whole next

Mel Torme recalled later. "Our dead president had not been in his grave three weeks . . . Garland had touched a responsive chord in every man and woman in the audience that night."

But no matter what Judy sang, her series remained at the bottom of the Nielsen ladder. The program stumbled along another few weeks and then, on January 23, Judy quit. She and CBS jointly announced that the series would be discontinued after the broadcast of March 29.

Judy and Ray Bolger reminisce about the making of *The Wizard of Oz* in 1963.

Judy, Liza, Lorna, and Joey share the spotlight on Mama's Christmas show in 1963.

There were still seven shows to complete, and Judy insisted that the next one to be taped be a one-woman concert. Included were nostalgic songs from the World War One era, patriotic tunes, and three tributes to people near and dear to Judy: "Liza," "Happiness Is Just a Thing Called Joe," and "Lorna's Song" (*The Judy Garland Show* opening theme, with special lyrics by Johnny Mercer).

Judy enjoyed this concert so much that three more were quickly added to the schedule, and generous doses of "just singing" were added to the other three shows, for which guests had already been contracted.

The twenty-sixth and final program was taped on Friday, March 13. Judy was disconsolate. Scheduled to start at 6:30 P.M., the session did not begin until 8:15—and continued with countless interruptions until 5:54 the next morning. Judy just did not want to say goodbye to a project on which she had pinned so many hopes. Only forty minutes of usable tape were completed that night. The remaining twenty had to be borrowed from an earlier telecast.

"My year in television was very enlightening—and funny," Judy commented later. "It was instant disaster. Sometimes instant success. It was that way every week, one way or the other. By the time we discovered where we were going, it was too late."

The series, however disappointing, did offer Judy an opportunity to work with great talents like Streisand, Peggy Lee, Lena Horne, Ethel Merman, and Count Basie. It gave fans the chance to hear Judy sing a vast assortment of new music.

She was asked if she would ever attempt another series. "No," she told *TV Guide*. "All in all the show was a good thing to have happen to me. I learned a great deal. But if I had known what I was in for, I would never have tried a weekly series. Not ever."

Judy had lost the Great Garland Gamble.

OVERLEAF: Judy rehearses a number, which was ultimately cut, for the final segment of her television series in 1964.

10

When she stands up there before an audience, she has the dignity of a woman who has been through it all and knows what it's all about. The people sense this new dignity and respond to it.

STANLEY KRAMER

nce again Judy was a vagabond vaudevillian. This time, however, the challenge was not so much to *attain* as merely to *sustain.*

In December 1963, an album of "reissues" entitled *The Hits of Judy Garland* was released, and in March 1964 numbers from the television soundtracks were packaged as *Just for Openers.* Capitol hoped the album would be successful enough to warrant sequels, but, like the series itself, it faltered.

Ray Aghayan, who had designed the costumes for Judy's show, introduced her to actor Mark Herron. With her marriage to Sid Luft continuing to disintegrate, Judy and Herron became constant companions.

In May, Judy attempted a tour of Australia and the Orient, but a much-anticipated performance in Melbourne ended in disaster: her voice gave out and fans booed when she cut the concert short. A week later, Judy's sister Susie committed suicide in Las Vegas, and Judy lay ill in a Hong Kong hospital.

Judy and Herron worked their way to London, and on July 23, she found acceptance once again at the Palladium. The occasion was the *Night of 100 Stars.* Judy had been hospitalized only days before with a bad cut on her arm, but she insisted on doing a walk-on. The audience refused to let her leave. "Sing,

Songs from Lionel Bart's *Maggie May* constituted Judy's final sessions with Capitol, but the records were never officially released in the United States (1964).

Judy, sing!" they shouted, and there were cries for "Over the Rainbow." Finally Judy relented: she sang both her theme song and "Swanee" and literally stopped the show. "The show ended," read one report, "in wild acclaim, with the Beatles and other stars massing around to congratulate her." "They went absolutely wild," a spokesman for the Palladium recalled. "I think if Judy hadn't sung the encore, there would have been a riot. When it was finished, it was impossible to do anything else, and the show simply had to end."

A few nights later, Judy indulged in a late-night recording session for Capitol, singing four tunes from Lionel Bart's new musical *Maggie May*.

Liza joined Judy and Mark in London in September for a week's vacation and then returned in November to start rehearsals for what would be their first—and only—mother-daughter concert, *Judy and Liza at the London Palladium*. Capitol put the evening on disc, and although Judy's performance was uneven at best, the record became a hit.

British television broadcast portions of the *Judy and Liza* concert in December, and Judy pretaped another segment for *The Jack Paar Show*. On this occasion, she chatted about her friend Marlene Dietrich and sang "What Now My Love?"

Once again Judy took to the road, singing at the O'Keefe Centre in Toronto, the Arie Crown Theater in Chicago, and the Fontainebleau in Miami. On February 5 she appeared as a talent scout on CBS's *On Broadway Tonight*, introducing audiences to Peter and Christopher Allen, a vocal duo she had met in the Orient. By this time, Peter was engaged to Liza.

"Mark found Chris and Peter in Hong Kong performing at a hotel," Judy explained. "I thought they were so good I put them under personal contract. We took them to London for our show there, and that's where Liza met Peter. They fell in love right away."

April 5 brought the annual Academy Awards telecast, and, although still frightened of "live" television, Judy agreed to sing a medley of Cole Porter

Program book from Judy and Liza's first joint concert at the London Palladium in 1965.

Judy salutes Cole Porter in a medley on the Academy Awards telecast in 1965.

BELOW: Loyal trouper and old friend Mickey Rooney joins Judy (sidelined with a broken elbow) on the stage of the Greek Theatre in Los Angeles.

hits. Judy was clearly not in top form; her performance was stiff, too intense, and not at all relaxed or controlled.

Judy's divorce from Sid Luft became final on May 14, 1965; in August, she confirmed plans to marry Mark Herron.

Hollywood had always been a good luck town for Judy's live concert performances, but that changed with her booking at the outdoor Greek Theater the week of September 13. Opening night was a triumph ("There is still magic in that voice," said one review), but later that evening she fell and broke her elbow in two places. The next evening Judy appeared on stage with her arm in a cast and, seated in a comfortable chair, attempted to sing. Mickey Rooney, Martha Raye, and Johnny Mathis came to her rescue and entertained during much of the evening.

On September 20, Judy appeared in an episode of *The Andy Williams Show*, and on October 3 she was in a Hollywood-based segment of *The Ed Sullivan*

Show. A couple of weeks later, she hosted an episode of the *Hollywood Palace* series, a program that aired November 13, the same day Judy and Mark were married in Las Vegas. None of Judy's children was present at the ceremony; Lorna and Joey were with their father, and Liza was in Los Angeles preparing to open November 22 at the Cocoanut Grove. The newlyweds rushed back to Hollywood to get a ring-side seat for Liza's opening night.

On December 17, Judy became the first pop singer to give a concert in Houston's fifty-thousand-seat Astrodome. Opening for her was an exciting new act from Detroit, the Supremes.

Spring brought more television—guest shots with Perry Como, Sammy Davis Jr., and, once again, the *Hollywood Palace.* After the Como broadcast, columnist Bob MacKenzie wrote, Judy "sounded fine and looked marvelous. Clad in a crazy cluster of black feathers, she was in good voice and was no more a bundle of nerves than was necessary to bring her now special drama to a ballad."

Judy's bundle of nerves erupted into a full-scale

Judy with fourth husband Mark Herron.

Just a little more above the lips: Judy clowns with her host on a segment of The Andy Williams Show.

problem on the *Hollywood Palace.* On the air, she looked fine, but the studio audience knew Judy was under a lot of pressure that night. She locked herself in her dressing room and for hours refused to come out. What people did not realize, until much later, was the reason. She and Herron were on the verge of separating. Nothing threatened Garland's self-assurance or spoiled a Garland performance more than a troubled love life. Needing an escort, Judy started appearing in public on the arm of the twenty-eight-year-old press agent Tom Green.

On March 3, 1967, Liza married Peter Allen in her agent's New York apartment. Judy surprised reporters by arriving with Vincente. Sid Luft was there with Lorna and Joey. Other guests included such close family friends as Tony Bennett, Yul Brynner, Phil Silvers, and Polly Bergen. "It was really the happiest, most relaxed wedding I've ever seen," Judy remarked proudly. "Of course, there were no strained relations between Vincente and me. . . . We're friends!"

While in New York, Judy appeared as the mystery guest on the *What's My Line?* game show and sat for an interview with Barbara Walters on the *Today* show. There was also a press conference to announce

Judy's return to motion pictures—in a film version of Jacqueline Susann's best-seller, *Valley of the Dolls.*

Judy's role was that of Helen Lawson, a hard-as-nails Broadway star supposedly patterned after Ethel Merman. Judy flew to Los Angeles and recorded "I'll Plant My Own Tree," a new song written for the film by Andre and Dory Previn.

Shooting started immediately at 20th Century-Fox Studios. Judy had her costume fittings and began to rehearse a fight scene with Patty Duke set in a women's bathroom. A week later Judy was fired.

Tom Green later confessed that once Judy had carefully studied the script, she wanted out and feigned illness: "Contrary to popular belief, Judy's departure from the *Valley* had nothing whatsoever to do with pills or liquor or tardiness. She was at the studio on time every day she was scheduled for filming . . . I wouldn't say that Judy's methods were exactly unquestionable, but her objective was a worthy one.

She at least managed to keep herself out of a dirty film." "I'm not Dorothy on the way to Oz any more," Judy explained, "but I'm not vulgar."

On April 11, Judy was granted a divorce from Mark Herron. At the judge's suggestion, she also made "Judy Garland" her legal name.

Judy and Sid were friends again, and he suggested they package a new television special of their own, a family affair produced by Sid, starring Judy, and featuring Lorna and Joe. He suggested a tour to try out new material.

"Mama had not worked for a while," Lorna recalled later, "and she really wanted to start again. My father came back at this point. He said, 'Judy, you just can't go on like this. Let me take over your career. I'll set up a tour for you.' Mama said she was ready, and things started to happen."

Luft set up an initial booking on the summer fair circuit. "It was fine," Judy joked later, "except for

ABOVE: Judy attends a press conference to announce her planned return to the movies in the film version of *Valley of the Dolls* (1965).

RIGHT: Judy belts a number on ABC's *Hollywood Palace.*

of "Me and My Shadow." Lorna sang a solo, and Joey did a number on the drums. To finish, Judy, Lorna, and Joey did a rousing chorus of "Together Wherever We Go."

"I was scared to death," Lorna admitted later. "Not just opening night, but every night of those four weeks—but, oh, I loved it!

"The audience was beautiful. Everybody was in tuxedos and gowns. Mama had rigged it so she would make her entrance from the back of the theatre. Her overture began and people went insane, totally insane. When that back door opened and she walked

Judy beams as she and her children Lorna and Joey Luft prepare to open on Broadway.

the bugs! Every night the stage looked like a battle-field."

Sid's plans for a family television special did not excite the major networks, so he suggested they do the show live on stage. What better place to begin than at Judy's favorite Manhattan theatre?

"Mama's face lit up like fireworks when Daddy told her," Lorna recalled, "because the Palace was her home. She called her writer and they began planning the act. Joey and I were to be part of it."

Judy Garland at Home at the Palace, staged by Richard Barstow, was another vaudeville variety show, featuring guests Jackie Vernon, John Bubbles, and Francis Brunn. Judy came on at the start of the second act. She sang alone and, with Bubbles, introduced Lorna and Joey for an old-soft-shoe version

Fans offer Judy gifts and flowers during her Christmas engagement at New York's Felt Forum.

down that aisle, it took her ten minutes to get to the stage. The first thing she said when she reached the stage was, 'I think I'm going to go out and come in again!' "

Vincent Canby, of the *New York Times*, called Judy a "female Lazarus . . . alive once again in New York City." He also found Garland's presence more important than her voice: "That the voice . . . is now a memory seems almost beside the point. . . . the Garland personality—wry and resilient—is intact . . . she was in fine fettle last night . . . in total command of the performance."

Judy's contract with Capitol had expired, so Sid made a deal for ABC-Paramount Records to record his family's first three Broadway evenings and release the highlights on a new album also called *Judy Garland at Home at the Palace.*

The show closed August 26, and Judy and the Lufts left New York for Boston, where she did a very successful free concert on the Boston Common. The next day Judy sang for patients at a nearby veterans hospital.

Judy and her children went on tour, giving nearly fifteen concerts between Labor Day and early November. Again Judy's lack of voice seemed less important than her very presence. "Her voice is a cracking carbon copy of those once vibrant pipes," wrote Bob Goddard in the *St. Louis Globe-Democrat,*

Judy returns to New York once again to headline at the Palace.

"but there's something about the big-name magic of this girl that still carries a compelling aura and authority that makes a Garland appearance a 'happening' even if it's not a songfest."

At the end of the tour, Joe and Lorna went back to New York. Lorna enrolled at the Professional Children's School. "Mama and Daddy were having a lot of trouble by then," she recalled later. "They split again. Mama was doing some concerts at the Garden State Arts Center in New Jersey. She was ill, and she cracked. Mama was hospitalized briefly, then went to Boston to visit a friend."

Judy's strength was running out. Performances were scheduled, often delayed an hour or more, occasionally canceled altogether "because of illness." The voice could be nearly perfect one night, gone the next. Rumors spread that some "fans" now bought tickets in the morbid hope that they would see her fail.

In the autumn of 1968, advertising executive Jane Trahey invited Judy to pose for one of the first in a series of advertisements she had conceived for Blackglama mink, a campaign to be called "What Becomes a Legend Most?"

On November 17, one legend saluted another when Judy appeared as the surprise guest star at a Lincoln Center tribute to Vincent Youmans, Noel Coward, and Harold Arlen. Honoring Arlen, Judy sang "The Man That Got Away," "It's a New World," "Get Happy," and "Over the Rainbow."

Judy had become friends with composer John Meyer, who began working with her and teaching her new compositions. His song "I'd Like to Hate Myself in the Morning" became a favorite, and Judy quickly added it to her repertoire.

In December, she made the rounds on the New York talk-show circuit (Dick Cavett, Johnny Carson, Merv Griffin) and accepted a five-week engagement at the Talk of the Town nightclub in London.

A new man had entered her life, musician and businessman Mickey Deans. On December 19, Judy announced their intention to marry. They flew to London on December 28 and were dismayed to discover that English law required a fifteen-day residency period before they could be legally wed. A further complication—Judy could not produce her final divorce papers from her marriage to Mark Herron. Finally, on March 15, the legal problems were settled, and in the ceremonial room of the Chelsea Registry Office, they were married.

Judy's engagement at the Talk of the Town proved to be another roller-coaster affair: Opening night was a genuine triumph, but later in the month, a performance ended with some rowdy patrons throwing empty cigarette packages at the stage when Judy arrived an hour late.

However, it was not in Judy's nature to stop trying. In March she and singer Johnnie Ray, who was Mickey's best man, teamed up for a show. "We toured together in Scandinavia and it was a big success, artistically and financially," he recalled. "I never had a difficult moment with her—we were too busy having fun."

Judy and Johnnie discussed taking their show to South Africa and Japan, but he had a five-week booking in Australia to complete first, so Judy and Mickey decided to fly to New York to visit friends and complete some unfinished business.

On June 15, the Deans flew back to London. Judy was as excited as ever about her future. Mickey had

John Meyer's "I'd Like to Hate Myself in the Morning" was the last new song to be added to Judy's repertoire and the last to be published bearing her picture.

Judy and her last husband, musician Mickey Deans, in 1968.

negotiated for a new television documentary, to be called *A Day in the Life of Judy Garland*, and Judy had started making lists of songs for a new concert. Johnnie Ray would be back soon, and maybe the two of them could. . . .

But there would be no documentary, no more concerts, no more radio shows or motion pictures or phonograph records. On June 22, Judy Garland, the little girl who sang "Jingle Bells" and took the world over the rainbow, died in her home in London from an accidental overdose of sleeping pills.

"The Scarecrow came to her funeral," reported *Time* magazine in 1969. "So did Andy Hardy. So in spirit did the countless legions of Judy Garland's fans, 21,000 of whom appeared in person . . . to file past the bier where her body . . . lay in state."

Not since the death of Rudolf Valentino had the world witnessed such an outpouring of affection for a deceased entertainer. Mourners stood for hours outside the Frank E. Campbell Funeral Parlor, waiting to say goodbye. Many were moved to tears when a girl from the Bronx began to play Judy's records on

Judy at London's Heathrow Airport in the year she died, 1969.

programs—came into renewed demand. Thanks to technology, much of her finest work will be available for generations to come.

This would please her greatly, since never has one performer given so much of herself for her craft. Some people work to live; Judy truly lived to work. She once said:

I think I'm most happy, when I'm entertaining people . . . making them forget their problems and worries.

You've heard aviators talk about the thrill of flying . . . how they feel when they get up there . . . the ship in their control. The earth drops away . . . they're alone in the sky. All the trivial things in life are forgotten. It isn't quite that they feel they are superior beings. It's just that all things ordinary and earthbound and tied up with the daily routine of living become insignificant beside the thrill and power of what they are doing.

That's the best way I can describe how I feel when I'm doing my job well . . . when I know I have the audience. I've felt it on the stage in vaudeville, in army camps, and hospitals. I've felt it come right through the mike on the air. When it happens before the camera and I notice carpenters and grips stop what they're doing to watch, I know I'm doing right and I'm happy.

Does that sound silly?

Not at all, Miss Garland.

a battery-powered phonograph. This seemingly insignificant incident was the first clue that Judy's magic would always be with us.

In the years immediately following her death, a spate of books appeared, each focusing on Judy's dark days, her battles with drugs and alcohol. Her popularity refused to wane, and, one by one, her performances—her films, recordings, and television

Judy's casket is taken from the Frank Campbell funeral parlor in 1969. In the forefront is the Reverend Peter Delaney, who conducted the services and, a few months earlier, had officiated at Judy's wedding to Mickey Deans.

"Goodnight, and God bless . . ."

INDEX*

*Italic page numbers denote locations of pictures.

117

119